MALAPROP THEATRE

Formed in 2015, MALAPROP Theatre is an award-winning collective of seven Dublin-based theatremakers: Carys D. Coburn, John Gunning, Breffni Holahan, Molly O'Cathain, Maeve O'Mahony, Claire O'Reilly and Carla Rogers.

Our work is bold, playful, and genre-spanning. We aim to challenge, delight and speak to the world we live in (even when imagining different ones).

Work to date includes *LOVE+*, *BlackCatfishMusketeer*, *JERICHO*, *Everything Not Saved*, *HOTHOUSE*, *GULP* (video), *Before You Say Anything* and *Where Sat the Lovers*.

The company has won the Spirit of Fringe Award (Dublin Fringe, 2015), Melbourne Fringe Award 2018, the Romilly Walton Masters Award 2018, and the Georganne Aldrich Heller Award (Dublin Fringe, 2017). We have performed our work in Ireland, the UK, France, China and Australia.

T0322400

MALAPROP
plays

Everything Not Saved
Before You Say Anything
Where Sat the Lovers
HOTHOUSE

NICK HERN BOOKS
London
www.nickhernbooks.co.uk

A Nick Hern Book

MALAPROP: plays first published in Great Britain as a paperback original in 2023 by Nick Hern Books Limited, The Glasshouse, 49a Goldhawk Road, London W12 8QP, in association with MALAPROP Theatre

MALAPROP: plays copyright © 2023 Carys D. Coburn with MALAPROP Theatre

The authors have asserted their moral rights

Cover photography by Pato Cassinoni; art direction by Molly O'Cathain

Designed and typeset by Nick Hern Books, London
Printed in Great Britain by Mimeo Ltd, Huntingdon, Cambridgeshire PE29 6XX

A CIP catalogue record for this book is available from the British Library

ISBN 978 1 83904 285 0

www.nickhernbooks.co.uk/environmental-policy

Contents

Introduction

It's been a busy few years since we were awarded Spirit of Fringe at Dublin Fringe Festival for *LOVE+*. At the time we weren't even a company, on the basis that a company name felt like a promise of a further show. We knew we could make *LOVE+* – because we'd just done so – but we didn't know if we could make something else.

And then, with the award, we suddenly had to! What a wonderful vote of confidence! What a terrifying vote of confidence!

It made sense, we felt, to take two years to make *Everything Not Saved*. So we could work out how we worked. To separate the idiosyncrasies of a single project – because they all have idiosyncrasies – from integral parts of the process. (*That* was a thing we did once, *this* is a thing we always do.) To work out our interests, goals, style.

Style, in particular, is a funny thing. Get too precious about it and you fall into self-parody. Get too self-conscious about getting too precious about it, and you risk alienating people who like your stuff by not doing things you want to do out of some vague sense you have a duty to 'innovate'. (Whatever that means.)

Our solution was not something we sat down and worked out. It was something that emerged from two years of intense work on everything else: *BlackCatfishMusketeer*, *JERICHO*, a truly bizarre short play that we performed at a corporate fundraising dinner. (The brief: okay, so, we're raising funds for children with haemophilia, so what if it was a retelling of the *Children of Lír* but instead of them turning into swans they had haemophilia and instead of their dad is a king who works for Construction Company We Can't Legally Name In This Introduction?)

We made shows that, in retrospect, we think share a set of priorities if not a set language. They all aim to say something about the world we live in, but to say it obliquely. To have the larger thought sneak up on you. Not because mystery is inherently more artistic, but so as to encourage reappraisal of what you thought you knew. To make you realise two disparate things are the perfect metaphor for each other. To make you think the sprawling, associative thought that you would not otherwise think.

In funding-application speak, we often say that we 'aim to challenge, delight and speak to the world we live in (even when imagining different ones)'. We're lucky to have found a moderately palatable soundbite that matches up moderately well with what we really think.

We also like this quote from Kim Stanley Robinson: 'If you want to write a novel about our world now, you'd better write science fiction, or you will be doing some kind of inadvertent nostalgia piece; you will lack depth, miss the point, and remain confused.'

That feels true to us. That realism is more 'radar ping' than 'Book of Revelation', a missive from where we've just been, a contingent truth subject to correction, a great flavour to round out a meal but never the main event. Grumio's totes hilarious joke from the *Shrew*: do you want the mustard without the beef?

'Contingent' is a good word. We like sci-fi because it's not not fantasy, because it reminds us that the present is future history and erstwhile future. Our pal Eoghan Quinn did a PhD with super-brainy cool dude Julia Jarcho, who talks about negating the present; there's a difference between *it is so* and *it is necessarily so*. That has a political charge, finding ways to get people to feel that the *givens* of the world are really *mades*. Not *data, facta*. It's the feeling of waking up on February 9th 2020 and Sinn Féin have seventeen Teachtaí Dála and Fianna Fáil and Fine Gael have one apiece. Not that we are Sinn Féin supporters, but this has never happened before! We might have the chance to be disappointed by the ostensibly left-wing party in government, instead of just swapping Fine Gael (capitalist death-cult) for Fianna Fáil (capitalist death-cult) until the end of time! Everything is where it was, but there's a new way through it all. It occurs to you that the same old dots can be joined in a different order. It occurs to you that taking a different path means new perspectives from new places we've never stood before.

Another quote we like, this from our fairy godmother Ali Smith: 'More and more, the pressing human dilemma: how to walk a clean path between obscenities.' That's the feeling, that there might be a clean path. You try not to feel it about electoral politics – most of us are the age that means our first election was the one that put Labour in power so Joan Burton could cut lone-parent benefits. We've been here before. And yet, and yet, the feeling of possibility. It's briefer and more doomed than the feeling of May 23rd 2015 or May 25th 2018, those big referendum results – there was actual hope on those days. Maybe the WHOLE country doesn't hate queers; maybe the WHOLE country doesn't hate women. But hope is a slippery instant between the months of terrified lead-up to the vote and the years of complex aftermath that have followed. Possibility is a less shiny feeling than hope, but it might be more durable. In the face of everything it is less of a strain to believe *it doesn't have to be this way* than *it gets better.*

Maybe that's the key to why we like sudden changes of subject that aren't. Maybe that's why the characteristic MALAPROP gesture – if there is one – is the zoom, whether out or in, movement without departure or arrival, things appearing or disappearing from where they weren't hiding but we couldn't see, sharpening or blurring until there's something there that wasn't there before. Hence the Queen, bad cops, Rasputin, bad cops again, nineteenth-century gays, seventeenth-century science and/or alchemy, Loughinisland, even more bad cops, Operation Legacy, immortal time-travelling drag king Isaac Newton, climate breakdown, rabbits, Blanchardstown, cruise ships, Minnie Riperton, great tits.

Enjoy.

EVERYTHING NOT SAVED

Carys D. Coburn
with MALAPROP THEATRE

Everything Not Saved was first performed at Project Arts Centre, Dublin, on 11 September 2017, as part of Dublin Fringe Festival. The cast was as follows:

B	Breffni Holahan
M	Maeve O'Mahony
P	Peter Corboy
SPOOKY-JEWEL-FACED- WOMAN-WHO-SHOOTS-B	Sara Gannon

Set, Costume, Graphic Design	Molly O'Cathain
Lighting Design	John Gunning
Sound Design	Brian Fallon
Stage Manager	Sara Gannon
Producer	Carla Rogers
Production Manager	Dara Ó Cairbre
Assistant Stage Manager	Ursula McGinn
Costume Assistant	Anna Chiara Vispi
Assistant Lighting Designer	Briony Morgan

Characters

B
M
P

Note on the Dialogue

Text in bold is voice-over and projection until it is indicated that the voice-over drops out. In the original production, the voice-over was progressively older in each section.

Where text is in [square brackets] these words are intended but unspoken.

One

Hi.

Thanks for coming.

Especially you, James.

What with the new baby and all.

Would you raise your hand if you wouldn't mind raising your hand in answer to some questions?

Please.

I'm asking nicely.

You don't have to, but it'll be more interesting if you do.

Thank you, everyone except the woman in the fifth row rolling her eyes.

Raise your hand if you think you'll remember, in five minutes, the face of the person who took your ticket?

If you think, in five minutes, you could draw that person from memory.

The man in the third row is lying.

Look at him there, with his beard and his lying hand.

Just, like, I mean, like, come ON, man in the third row. Don't lie.

Maybe I should try to be more ingratiating.

Maybe you'd find this easier if you could see someone.

Would you raise your hand if there's a photo of you you really hate?

If you'd be embarrassed if, after your death, that photo was the only image remaining of you?

If you feel like that photo doesn't really represent all of who you are in any meaningful sense?

If you feel like all of the photos of you ever taken still don't accomplish that?

Because that's the problem, isn't it?

Photos only show what you looked like that one time.

And you've looked like lots of other things too.

Including shit.

Video is arguably better for that.

Capturing change over time.

Your words. Your actions.
Not just how you looked but how you sounded.
That one time anyway.
But you still have to choose what to capture.
Because an unedited video of your whole life would be as
long as your whole life.
And it would take someone else's whole life to watch your
whole life.
And who'd do that?
Who, if anyone, loves you that much?
Maybe you're thinking 'perspective?!'.
Well done. Top marks. Your medal's in the post.
There's always a perspective the camera hasn't covered.
Yours.
Because the camera isn't your eyes, unless you're a robot.
But you're not a robot.
Don't lie.

Say everyone recorded their whole life. Whose life, if
anyone's, would you want to watch?

Throughout this section, a garden with a small iron table and
chair has been constructed on the stage in full view of the
audience. It should vaguely resemble the garden in Cape Town
from which Queen Elizabeth II made an address when she was
still Princess Elizabeth, on the occasion of her birthday. M has
also entered, dressed as Princess Elizabeth, with her printed
speech in her hands. She seats herself at the table poisedly.

Best Bits

M. Now that we are coming to manhood and womanhood, it is
   surely a great joy to us all to think that we shall be able to take
   some of the burden off the shoulders of our elders who have
   fought, and worked, and suffered to protect our childhood.

   I hope you didn't put your hand up for that question, it
   wasn't yes or no, that would be silly.

M. We must not be daunted by the anxieties and hardships that the
   war has left behind in every nation of our Commonwealth.

Say only one photo of one person from one time will survive the nuclear war next year.

What do you hope that photo is?

M. We know that these things are the price that we cheerfully undertook to pay for the high honour of standing alone seven years ago, in defence of the liberty of the world.

Say it's the year before the Queen died, I'm sure you all remember that.

M. Let us say with Rupert Brooke: 'Now God be thanked who has matched us with his hour.'

And we're here, with them, in their friend's garden.

B *and* P *take up their places in the scene;* B *behind* M *with her camera on a tripod, and* P *off to one side with a reflector such that it's uncertain whether he exists.*

M. I am sure that you will see our difficulties in the light that I see them; as the great opportunity for you and me.

B. Bit slower.

M. I thought you weren't recording audio.

B. I'm not but when you talk like a normal person, you move like a normal person.

M. Which is too fast.

B. Yeah.

M. Sorry. Are you recording this?

B. Yeah.

M. So I should stop talking?

B. Yeah.

M. Like now?

B. Yeah.

M. Are you getting cross?

B. Yeah.

M. Is there any chance you'll go to jail?

B. For this?

M. Yeah.

B. No.

M. Is it not though a bit –

B. What?

M. Y'know.

B. Unethical?

M. Profoundly unethical.

B. No.

M. You sure?

B. Very.

M. So, the Queen dies.

B. Statistically, within four years.

M. And then the media go apeshit.

B. Queenarama.

M. Lizapalooza.

B. Extrazabethaganza.

M. Just the fucking dead Queen, like, everywhere.

B. Yeah.

M. Highlights of her reign.

B. Momentous moments.

M. Her trying not to look guilty when Diana died.

B. Trying not to look awkward when her boyfriend was racist.

M. The different coins. The coins have been different, haven't they?

B. Yeah.

M. So that's what you're, what we're doing?

B. Queen footage?

M. For TV.

B. For when she dies?

M. Yeah.

B. Yeah.

M. Even though we're not English.

B. To the continuing shock of English people.

M. Yeah.

B. Yeah. Work is work, though.

M. And I'm not the Queen.

B. Wait, WHAT?!

M. I feel like you go to jail for not being the Queen.

B. You won't go to jail.

M. I don't know laws, but aren't there laws?

B. You definitely won't go to jail.

M. Funny. I just assumed it wasn't people.

B. Making or editing the – ?

M. Yeah. Privately. That it was a government thing.

B. Well, in North Korea it would be.

M. Oh, right. Yeah.

B. Because what you're describing is propaganda.

M. Yeah.

B. But, in fairness, I sometimes forget that that's bad.

M. Media monopolies?

B. Feels like a sailed ship when Google owns everyone's tits and dicks.

M. Everyone's tits and dicks?

B. Literally everyone's titties and dickies.

M. Shit.

B. Yeah.

M. And this is before the Queen was the Queen?

B. Yeah. This is Princess Elizabeth on her twenty-first birthday in 1947. Turn around for a sec…

M. Seventy years ago.

B. Good maths.

M. Just after the war.

B. Good history.

M. Mad, isn't it?

B. Time?

M. Just like, time yeah.

B. There's footage of her giving this speech from Cape Town.

M. I'm finding this weird.

B. Sitting on a chair at a table in a garden just like this.

M. Being dressed as the Queen.

B. The war had only been over two years.

M. With her filming me.

B. Twenty-one and engaged. If I'd married who I was with when I was twenty-one, I'd be married to her.

M. I remember the last time I wore this necklace was to a dinner party here.

B. Don't get me wrong, but FUCK.

M. And, while I was getting ready, she kept trying to take a photo of me. Naked.

B. Like, now I think I like my photos of her better than I like her.

M. And I couldn't move. Literally.

B. One in particular. Where she's facing the camera naked.

M. Because I had my hand over the lens and I didn't trust her not to take my photo if I took it away.

B. From when she was, or we, or, actually, things maybe weren't complicated. Less so, anyway.

M. And I started feeling a bit scared. Of having to have the fight we would have to have if she did.

B. She was shy back then, but that's why I like it. Having a memory of that shyness.

M. Because she'd win.

B. And the act of making the memory helped her not be. Shy any more.

M. So I kept saying STOP.

B . Why?

M. Because I feel like, at any moment, you're going to shove your dick in my mouth.

B. I don't think that's fair.

M. Because you don't have a dick?

B. Because I'm not some creep with a shit moustache who says there's a modelling job when there isn't.

M. Then stop acting like one.

B. One photo.

M. Fuck off.

B. Super tasteful.

M. Fuck off.

B. Bush but no lip.

M. Fuck right off.

B. And you can cover your nips with your hand – You hesitated!

M. No I didn't.

B. Bush and covered nips, then I'll leave you alone forever.

M. Forever?

B. Forever.

M. Forever?

B. Forever.

P. This is actually my garden, and it's so good to have them both here again.

M. Standing?

B. Whatever.

P. It's not that I took sides; there aren't sides.

M. Sitting?

B. Whatever.

P. But we'd never learned how to talk to each other one on one.

M. Standing then.

B. Okay then.

P. I find that pretty difficult generally actually; talking one on one.

M. How's this?

B. Perfect.

> P *now definitely exists, and his reflector becomes a tray of G and Ts with cucumber in them.*

P. I have drinks with cucumber in them!

M (*with a self-aware quoting air*). I mean of COURSE cucumber!

B. We're real people.

P. Your Majesty.

M (*in her Queen voice*). One is very grateful.

B. I definitely told you I wouldn't be recording audio.

P. Any excuse.

M. ANY excuse.

B. To do voices?

P (*in a voice*). To do voices.

M (*in a non-Queen voice*). To do voices.

B. What the fuck was that meant to be?

P. Why are you not recording audio of her amazing Queen impression?

M. It's actually Princess Elizabeth, actually, on her birthday in – 1946?

B. Seven.

P. Seventy years ago.

M. I did that because six is green.

B. What?

P. Weird, it's red for me.

M. Because we're in the garden.

B. Wait, WHAT?

P. That cucumber's gone STRAIGHT to your head.

M. So when I thought about what you said a minute ago I was getting green, but it was the plants. But I thought it was the number, and green is six. Six is the green number. Mad that it's not for you, is it for you? So, that's why I thought that you had said – thought that it was six.

B. It's seven, though.

P. It's really great to see you both again!

M. It is.

B. Properly.

P. I mean, it must be –

M. Like, what?

B. Two years since that lunch?

P. It can't be.

M. Time.

B. Yeah, because the election was –

P. Yeah, fuck. Which means that that dinner was –

M. Four?

B. Nearly five years ago.

P. I want to say his name was Jake?

M. From that dinner?

B. Your boy?

P. Who I had that, a date ends up being a whole weekend, instant, y'know, chemical-level-attraction-type thing with. With whom.

M. Who stayed to dinner with us.

B. And ended up being a total dick.

P. Who liked working for a startup.

M. And ended everything he said with *speaking personally*.

B. Not even *personally speaking*.

P. That was weird.

M. Like, what else –

B. Would he be speaking as?

P *(in a fantastical ambassadorial voice)*. ON BEHALF OF MY PEOPLE.

M *(in a fantastical ambassadorial voice)*. ON BEHALF OF THE GALACTIC COUNCIL.

B. What the fuck was that meant to be?

P. I feel strongly one syllable?

M. Like Jake?

B. Dave?

P. Dave was the activist.

M. Who had a dick.

B. What did we think his dick was, again?

P. Friendly?

M. With the friendly dick.

B (*in a voice*). Enchanté. Voices.

> *At some point during the ensuing text, a member of stage*
> *management brings out some comically sketchy representation*
> *of the Dumb Hot Jock and gives it to P to help him illustrate his*
> *memory of the dinner. In our production, he was a mannequin*
> *head attached to the top of a broom handle. Whatever he is, it's*
> *key that he be obviously less detailed than a real man.*

P. But yes he turned out to be a total dick, whatever his name was,
not Dave, who just had one, a dick, and not friendly, unlike
Dave's. And I think he had a kind of a Dumb Hot Jock face, like
the character who, in a movie set in an American high school,
says things like Hey, SECOND NAME, nice SHIRT to the
protagonist after squirting ketchup all over said shirt, meaning
protagonist can't ask hot popular Mandy Spoopelpeim to the
Sadie Hawkin's dance. That happens a lot in films, though I
actually can't name a single specific one where that happens
right now. Maybe if I saw him right now, I'd be surprised by
how normal he looks. Maybe I'm remembering him as more
Dumb-Hot-Jock-looking than he was because he acted that
way too, but he definitely looked at least a bit Dumb Hot Jock,
because I have and had a bit of a guilty thing about that like
hmm, in school you definitely would have bullied me but instead
we're naked, deadly, I must be growing as a person or at least
getting better at hiding my sad breakable true self under a sexy
veneer.

And then, at dinner, we were sitting here in this garden, the four
of us, and you were all –

M. Something about the election.

P. And he said how he felt something kind of snide and patronising
about people with left-leaning politics and no money, speaking
personally, which made everything a bit awkward. And then you
were all –

B. Retaliatory snideness about people with centre-right politics who would have been Nazis in Nazi Germany, followed up with a casual reference to my then current photo exhibition people were liking, so he would know I was successful, also because I was going through that real arrogant phase where my successes didn't make me happy because I obviously deserved them, and so much more, which you were hoping I would come out of and I did.

P. And I was kind of waiting for you to be all –

M. Affectionate teasing about your persecution and or god complex.

P. But instead, you just kind of stood there looking bored. And I remember thinking Shit, are they alright? I'd never thought you'd break up until right then. I'd just assumed we'd always be doing this, the three of us, plus David or this guy who is maybe Jake or whoever, and so I had a moment where I just thought Shit.

M. And then to stop you talking about your exhibition I started saying how photos aren't actually memories, because I've had photos of my dad for more years than I've had my dad at this stage, and they still look weird to me because you don't look at photos every day. Or I don't, maybe you do. But also because I look and think Weird, he's so small, he's like the same height as my mother who I'm taller than now, but to me his face was always up here, so somewhere I still think that's how tall he was even though he wasn't, I've just gotten bigger. That being kind of how it works over time, you get bigger, but you remember things as though you've always been the same size and everything else has changed. I mean, imagine if my dad was actually this tall!

That's what I was saying.

And then I was talking about Diana? Because of how I'd been sitting on my dad's lap playing with the buttons on his coat when the news was on the telly, and because I remember finding those buttons SO HUGE. Like just WHAT?! Are these buttons even POSSIBLE?!

The whole coat, actually, I used to wear it as a cape and it would brush the floor, it was the biggest, the warmest thing. Or if we were driving home late he'd wrap me in it and I'd feel like an egg or something, and I still have this really vivid feeling of having that coat all over me and just seeing streetlights move across my closed eyes that way they do that it seems they're getting faster, but actually it's just that light intensity increases faster than distance decreases, which feels like getting faster.

Obviously that's not something I knew when I was a tiny child, just like I didn't know then that it was sad Diana was dead. But I can't not think that now when I remember those lights, just like I can't not know that it was sad Diana was dead, just like I can't not think now that the last thing Diana saw was probably something like those lights going by.

I have to remind myself that that's just me, that that's not what happened.

That's what I was saying.

At the dinner party.

That photos aren't my memories.

Because, in my memories, my dad is eight feet tall and his coat is a cape and the last thing Diana saw was what I saw when I was a tiny child.

Photos remind me to remember, but they're not my memories.

So, why do we love them so much?

Why do we have that urge to make records?

Why do we kill people in tunnels with that urge?

And now all we remember of her is that she died that one time.

Even though she did lots of other things too, to me, she's just this woman who's always been dead.

That's just so weird.

That's what I was saying.

That I find records, photos, and videos, and stories just so weird.

That remembering things always changes them, even if it doesn't always kill them.

And I asked you did that ever bother you, the morality of it, as a photographer and film-maker, and you were all –

B. Something glib about never having murdered anyone in a tunnel on secret orders from the Queen.

M. You'd be a much better artist if you weren't so glib so people would like you. Those were my actual words. I remember because they were so harsh. You'd be a much better artist if you weren't so glib so people would like you. And then passing it off as a joke that came out too harsh, which you didn't really buy! And then you were all –

B. Playing along that it was a joke so as to look like I'm not so arrogant that I can't find mockery sincerely funny, even though back then I AM so arrogant that I can't find mockery sincerely funny!

M. And then, he said GAS, Hot Dumb Jock guy said GAS, shit's after getting real intellectual and shit, is that just me? That's what I think, speaking personally.

Those were his exact words. I remember.

Do you remember him saying that?

Simultaneously, syncing at the start and finish but desyncing in the middle where the memories diverge, aware it's happening but helpless to stop it:

When he said GAS, shit's after getting real intellectual and shit, is that just me, that's what I think, speaking personally, didn't he?

P. Yeah, he said GAS, that was some real brainy carry-on or shit, I mean am I wrong, that's my take, speaking personally, didn't he?

B. Yeah, he said GAS, shit's after getting super-nerdy and shit, don't you think, I mean do, speaking personally, didn't he?

P. And then he pretended to smoke a joint, which I fucking HATE.

M. Me too.

B. Me too.

P. Like, wow.

M. Thanks for the non-fucking-contribution.

B. Though he was the one started us putting cucumber in drinks.

P. Because when I said, Cucumber? He said I mean, of COURSE cucumber.

M. Which is why I said I mean, of COURSE cucumber!

B. That's why that's a thing.

P. Because he'd pretended to smoke a joint because he thought we WE were pretentious.

M. But he insisted on putting cucumber in drinks.

B. You don't get to do both those things.

P. Did you say why you're not recording audio?

M (*in her Queen voice*). One wishes to know.

B. I'm not recording audio because all I need is the over-the-shoulder shot we've been shooting, so I can splice it into the actual footage of Baby Liz in Cape Town in 1947.

P. To put into a press package?

M. For when the Queen dies.

B. For when the Queen dies and she's everywhere.

P. And you'll sell this press package to TV stations?

M (*in a voice*). For ONE MILLION DOLLARS?

B (*in a voice*). For ONE MILLION DOLLARS.

P. Funny. I just assumed it wasn't people.

M. Me too!

B. It's people.

P. Can you go to jail for not being the Queen?

M. I don't know laws, but she says no.

B. Even if people notice, no.

P. So, I've loaned you my garden for a project no one's going to notice?

M. You didn't tell me it wasn't going to be noticed.

B. It won't be noticed, but it'll make a difference.

P. Is that clever or made up?

M. The cucumber's gone STRAIGHT to her head.

B. It'll feel more intimate.

P. Than?

M. The original?

B. The original.

P. Is this not a lot of effort still?

M. Nonetheless.

B. There are worse things than an afternoon with the two of you.

P. Flirt.

M. Flirt.

B. Definitely better than sixteen hours in an editing studio.

P. Flirt.

M. Flirt.

B. Y'know, trying to keep up with everything the Queen is still doing because she's alive still.

P. Flirt.

M. Okay!

B. Which you can't do, keep up, unless you made a film of her ninety-something-year-long life that was itself ninety-something-years long.

    And no one would watch that.

    So sooner or later you have to start picking details.

    And this is me trying to pick the right ones.

    So that we don't just remember her as that queen who was old that one time.

    Because she was lots of other things too.

    And it's only interesting that she was so old because she was once so young.

But that's what people will forget the fastest.

Unless they see her young thin neck, shot from behind.

Unless they see her hands trembling as she holds her notes.

Unless they see her take a deep breath to steady them.

B *shepherds* M *back into Queen position, possibly with a shot-ruining G and T somewhere in shot.*

P. Even if they're her hands?

M. Even if they're my hands?

B. The image isn't a lie because the image isn't a memory.

P. No?

M. No?

B. No. (*Taking the piss out of her own pretension.*) The image is the ticket and memory's the journey.

(*Forgetting to pretend to be self-aware.*) Or it's a place. Memory. Memory is a place in a forest or something where you'd need a path, and if you don't go to it often enough, then the path disappears and you can't get back to it.

So you have to make the pilgrimage, which is what this is.

M. That was very sincere!

B. Trying not to be glib.

Who was it remembered that thing about him saying speaking personally? Was it you?

P. I don't know.

M. I think it was me.

B. But could you say for sure?

P. Like one hundred per cent certainty?

M. one hundred per cent

B. Yeah.

P. I think, but no.

M. I think, but no.

B. And now I'm going to remember that you did. Even if you didn't. Just because you said you did.

P. Spooky.

P pretends to smoke a joint.

M. Do you still have that photo of me?

B. I have lots of photos of you.

M. From when we had that fight.

B. Sorry?

M. Before here.

B. Before the dinner?

M. The one where I'm –

B. Oh yeah, yeah, I do. What fight though?

M. Seriously?

B. I genuinely have no idea what you mean.

M pauses, then begins her text again rather than speak.

M. I declare before you all that my whole life, whether it be long or short, shall be devoted to your service, and to the service of our great imperial family to which we all belong, but I shall not have strength to carry out this resolution alone, unless you join in it with me, which I now invite you to do.

Two

In five hours, do you think you could tell someone what happened in this show, start to finish?
In five hours, do you think you'll remember our names from the one time we said them at the very start?
In five hours, do you think you'll have forgotten something and not know?

In five hours, do you think you'll misremember something
and not know?
Because that's the problem, isn't it?
That happens so much.

I mean, I remember breaking my sister's nose when we were
six and feeling really guilty.

But I also remember my twin breaking MY nose.
And my twin remembers both those things, too.
And our noses look basically the same.

As you can see.
Because the breaking of the nose only happened once.

Whoever it belonged to.
But the story of the breaking of the nose has been told lots of
times.

We've more memories of what we've said about what
happened than OF what happened.
And we've both said things about having the nose and
breaking the nose, so we both remember both.
And our parents don't know.
Or can't say with one hundred per cent certainty, anyway.
Which doesn't reflect well on them.
Weird, right? The whole thing?
How brains can't be trusted because they never show us the
same thing twice.
Like how yours maybe thought you'd forgotten the bit
where we said our names at the start.
But actually, we never said our names.
You only thought you'd forgotten, if you thought for even
a split second you'd forgotten, because I said we'd done
something we hadn't.
Basically we're saying brains can't be trusted because brains
trust words.
And words can't be trusted either.

Forensic Actor

P *is seated on a chair, while* B *hovers around him.* M *is observing from a short distance such that it's not clear if she exists.*

B. Did you pick her up? Did you rock her?

P. She's a baby. Yes, at some point, yes, I picked her up.

B. So, then what? What did you do then?

P. I told you. I went downstairs and watched TV until Joanne and Colin came home.

B. Which was when?

P. About midnight?

B. So, you're telling me between ten thirty and midnight you just watched TV, you didn't go upstairs once. I mean, what are they even paying you for?

P. No. I mean yes, that's what I did, no I didn't go upstairs again.

B. You were just watching TV?

P. Yeah, and on my phone.

B. Were you talking to someone on your phone?

P. I don't know. You can check. I was probably messaging Dara or Carl or something – about homework? – I can't remember –

B. What if I told you your prints match the bruising? And all of a sudden, at that point, you go Now what? I mean, what are you gonna do?

P. At that point I would go I don't know, because I don't remember. I don't remember any of the things you're telling me I did.

B. Is it possible she wasn't okay at ten thirty p.m.? Is it possible you may have hurt her?

P. I don't know, I don't –

B. You don't know, okay. You don't know. Can you tell me it's totally impossible that you hurt her? Is it totally impossible? Are you one hundred per cent certain that you didn't do anything that might have in some way hurt her?

P. I don't know.

B. Even by accident? Was it an accident?

P. You're getting inside my head.

B. If it was an accident, if you did this accidentally, we can talk about that, but if we find out you did this and you don't tell us, we can't help you. I can't help you, okay?

P. Okay.

B. Do you remember rocking her at ten thirty?

P. Yes.

B. Do you think you may have done something accidentally to hurt her at that time.

P. Maybe, I – yeah, maybe.

B. Okay, thank you very much for your co-operation.

A break, where B *relaxes for the first time since the questioning began. Where we might expect* P *to look crushed or exhausted, he instead also relaxes. Maybe he stretches.* B *looks to* M.

M. How do you think that went?

B. –

Yeah?

M. What if I told you the suspect is innocent and you just elicited a false confession?

B. But you told me, though, to get a confession from him before we started, though.

M. Yeah.

B. That he was guilty.

M. Yeah. How often do you think, in real life, you'll get to be that certain?

B. Fuck.

M. When, if ever, do you think you'll trust your boss that much?

B. Fuck. Yeah.

M. It's almost like there's a reason we don't assume people are guilty until proven otherwise.

B. Yeah.

M. Are you cross at me?

B. Yeah.

M. Are you glad this is an exercise and not an actual case though?

B. Yeah.

M (*to* P). Anything else?

P. –

    Me?

M. Anything to add?

P. Eh – No?

M (*to* B). Tell me about one hundred per cent certainty.

B. Yeah?

M. Do you think that's a test a teenager, a teenager under stress will pass? That anyone is ever able to pass?

B. I don't know.

M. Five minutes ago, did you ask him about his texts before or after you asked him about the parents?

B. Okay, yeah.

M. I'm going to make you answer though; texts or parents first?

B. Texts.

M. Are you one hundred per cent certain?

B. No.

M. Are you one hundred per cent certain that you're not saying you asked about texts before parents because I said texts before parents?

B. No.

M. We'll leave that there. Take five and then we'll do scenario B.

B. Okay, thanks.

> B *leaves the stage and there is a break, in which it would be weirder for* P *and* M *to not look at each other than to look at each other, after which it would be weirder not to say anything than to say something.*

M. Phew!

P. Phew!

M. Okay?

P. Yeah, all good.

M. You do this all the time, I suppose.

P. Yeah.

M. Can I get you a glass of water, or – ?

P. I'm fine, I actually have one, or, a bottle, anyway, actually.

M. Cool. Long day!

P. Yeah.

M. But only, I want to say, two? Two left.

P. And it's Aaron for both?

M. Aaron?

P. Sorry, the kid. I use Aaron for the child – the younger child.

M. Yeah, the kid for the woman you just did babysitter with and then the child again for the guy from earlier.

P. Cool.

M. Do you want me to set anything up for you?

P. Like types of questions or her thinking the babysitter is guilty?

M. Yeah or any precautions or – ?

P. No, thank you.

M. You sure?

P. Thanks, yeah, but I'm fine. It's about what's useful for them.

M. To know going in?

P. Or find out, about the case, about procedure with small kids. I mean, what do you want them to know going in?

M. Yeah, I'll give them the situation they're walking into, but procedure for the child, I think it's better to just let them work it out?

P. It?

M. The rules, the rules out.

P. Cool.

M. If I can ask…

P. Yeah?

M. How did you get into this?

P. Forensic acting?

M. If I can ask.

P. Yeah! A friend does it in hospitals for doctors of mine, a friend of mine, and it's time flexible, and the money's better than my restaurant job, and I enjoy it more.

M. Enjoy?

P. Not enjoy. Fuck, that sounds –

M. No, I know what you mean.

P. It feels more worth doing.

M. And it's your skills.

P. Acting?

M. Yeah.

P. Yeah.

M. I'd say you're great in things when you're in things. Do you have a favourite?

P. Character?

M. If that's the right –

P. Yeah. I mean, 'favourite'?

M. Fair.

P. But I prefer babysitter.

M. Really?

P. Yeah, he's older. When you're doing a small child – fuck, that sounds –

M. No, I know what you mean –

P. But still –

M. Unfortunate –

P. Very unfortunate. When you're in character as a small child, it's hard to remember to not understand things or, you know, because I do, because I'm not. A small child, I mean.

And I prefer being a suspect.

M. Yeah?

P. Less, I don't know, draining or something.

M. Funny, that's the opposite.

P. Of?

M. I suppose I thought actors would like being victims.

P. Oh.

M. Is that insulting?

P. No.

M. Are you just being polite, though, because it's an insulting thing to say.

P. Really, no.

M. Objectively, that actors are insecure people and like doing big emotion because it makes them feel important, that's objectively insulting to say.

P. I mean, you didn't say that until just there.

M. But you didn't think I did?

P. Really, really, really wasn't insulted.

M. Oh, good.

P. And I kind of agree.

M. Agree?

P. With what you didn't say about actors.

M. Oh, yeah?

P. Or, more broadly, people who haven't had bad things happen to them. Who feel like it makes you interesting, having suffered, so they seek it out, or, like to borrow it? If they're actors.

M. But not all actors.

P. Not all actors.

M. Not you?

P. Not me, nothing to prove.

M. Which is why you weren't insulted.

P. Yeah.

M. Because you – ?

P. Sorry?

M. No I'm – forget I said anything.

P. Okay?

M. Because that's not something you can ask.

P. I mean, you didn't ask me anything.

M. No, thankfully.

P. Thankfully?

M. Because it would be so rude. And in a work context, just like Hey, tell me all about the formative experiences that make you tick and continue to inform your life in far-reaching ways without any, I don't know, consideration of –

P. Ohhhh.

M. Yeah. See, you can't just ask someone –

P. If their past is fucked.

M. Yeah.

P. If my past is fucked.

M. Yeah. Sorry.

P. No, you're fine. And it is.

M. Sorry?

P. My past. Fucked. I don't mind saying so.

M. Oh.

P. Even though you didn't ask.

M. Right. You're sure I can't get you a coffee?

P. Did you offer me coffee?

M. Didn't you say no?

P. Was that not water?

M. I'm sure I offered you coffee.

P. Because I would actually quite like coffee.

M. Weird, sorry, did you not say no?

P. To water.

M. Are you sure?

P. Maybe you did.

M. Weird.

P. Not one hundred per cent.

M. I can get you coffee.

P. If you don't mind.

M. Milk?

P. Just black, thanks.

M *leaves to get* P'*s coffee, and* P *begins to warm up for the next session. He gradually adopts the physicality he uses for Aaron.*

When I'm five –

When I'm five, I don't make eye contact.

When I'm five, I can't really answer sequential questions like What happened on Tuesday?

If you ask me did I eat dinner with my dad before going swimming, I'll say yes, but only because you're nodding while you ask.

My memory is fragments of coloured glass or shiny beads.

It's not a stained-glass window or a necklace.

It has quality but no pattern.

I don't know when things happened, but I know how I felt about them.

I know what I like and don't like.

And I need to be asked about two or three things I like, safe topics, before I'll answer questions about the things I don't like.

Even then, I'll stop talking unless reassured I won't get in trouble.

Preferably two or three times.

And all of that has to happen in less than twenty minutes, both legally and practically.

M *re-enters with a coffee cup for* P.

M. Coffee!

P. Thanks.

M. This must be really hard for you.

P. The job?

M. Given, or, in light of –

P. Stuff?

M. It must make you think of things. Remind you.

P. Well, yeah.

M. Is that not hard?

P. Yeah, but, equally, it sounds like you're assuming real life doesn't remind me.

M. Oh yeah.

P. But it does.

M. Well, thank you.

P. For?

M. Telling me.

P. Oh.

M. God, I'm not saying thank you for –

P. For having been abused as a child?

M. Oh, so that was it? Sorry. What I mean is –

P. Yeah?

> B *has re-entered and is ready to begin again.* M *takes the easy way out.*

M. Ready to go?

B. Yeah.

> B *takes a seat opposite* P.

Hi there.

P. Hi.

B. What's your name?

P. Aaron.

B. Aaron?

P. Yeah.

B. Hi Aaron, it's very nice to meet you. Thanks for talking to me today. How old are you, Aaron?

P. Five.

B. So are you in second class? Have I got that right?

P. No.

B. Oh okay. What class are you in?

P. Emer's class.

B. Emer's class, okay. Is that junior infants?

P. Senior infants.

B. Oh okay. And do you like school?

P. When I'm ten, my memories are more narrative.

B. What do you like?

P. My new memories anyway.

B. Me too. Which one's your favourite?

P. My memories of being five, from half my life ago, are shaped by how and when I've remembered them since.

B. Are you a fast runner?

P. The questions I was asked and the answers I gave.

B. Who's the fastest runner in your class?

P. If I've been asked the wrong questions, in the wrong way, I'll remember things wrongly.

B. Is Rory your friend?

P. Or not at all.

B. Is he your best friend?

P. This might mean someone who shouldn't go to prison does.

B. Does Rory like school?

P. This might mean someone who should go to prison doesn't.

B. That's okay, take your time.

P. In fact, it does mean both those things, often.

B. Do you like Emer?

P. When I'm fifteen, I have more memories of talking about being five than I do of being five. Twice as many in fact.

B. Does Rory like Emer?

P. The details of the story I tell when I have to tell it, to lawyers or new girlfriends, no longer feel like what happened felt.

B. You can tell me.

P. My memory has split in two. It is a story I feel to be false and a feeling I know is true.

B. What secrets?

P. When I'm twenty, other people's stories feel more like that feeling than my own story does. Odd things make my heart pound. The smell of a disinfectant. A particular bus route.

When I'm twenty-five, I hear a story about an American woman who survived a school shooting twenty years ago and recently realised she doesn't like to wear heels to parties because it means she won't be ready to run.

And I think, yeah.

I think, part of you is always waiting for something bad to happen.

But if you seek out the feeling it can't sneak up on you.

When I'm thirty, I spend six hours a week with dysfunction. It's not my dysfunction, I wouldn't do it if it was. It's not what happened, but it feels like what happened felt.

I don't feel like I'm wallowing. I feel like I'm acknowledging.

I feel like if I have no choice but to remember. It's nice to have a time and a place where I'm not just allowed to, but supposed to, and in the hopes that others won't have to.

It's a controlled fall.

A bungee jump, if you like.

Three

In five days, do you think you'll remember what year Queen
Elizabeth delivered her speech in?
Sorry. Princess. Princess Elizabeth.

In five days, do you think you'll remember the name of the
person in the audience who had the new baby?
Sorry. Babies.
Because you had twins, didn't you?
Or YOU didn't, stupid man. Your partner did; fair fucks to
her.
It's all ahead for you.
I should know, speaking as one; a twin.

I'm a twin because my mother had us after she turned
thirty-five.
That's a thing. Look it up.
Your body, or maybe not your body, but women's bodies,
after thirty-five are like
LAST CHANCE TO BREED! PUMP OUT THE FUCKING
TWINS!
She wasn't sure for years if she wanted kids at all.
Because her mother – my grandmother – had her so young
and it kind of fucked her life up.

That being the time.
People settled down earlier.
And her mother – my great-grandmother – had her and,
like, a million other kids too young.
That also being the time.
Having a million kids.
Her sister, on the other hand, didn't.
My great-grand-aunt, if that helps.
She didn't because the only time she got pregnant was before
she was married.
And the child didn't survive labour.
And while she was exhausted, devastated, still under
anesthesia, only twenty, doctors prevailed upon her to sign a
form.
She didn't realise she was consenting to a tubal ligation.

And even if she had realised, she didn't know it meant permanent sterilisation.

They recommended it on the grounds of 'a predisposition to immorality'.

Seeing as she wasn't married.

That also being the time.

I remember these people because they're my family.

So it's my job.

And part of that job is to remember my great-grand-aunt, because if I don't, no one will.

The problem being all I know about her is that there is no one else to remember her.

Which is not much better than being forgotten.

Being remembered just for the worst thing that happened to you.

But then that's history.

All that fucked-up stuff that happens to all of us.

If it's everyone's job to remember their family, whose job is it to remember the stuff that happened to everyone?

Is it everyone's job?

Do you trust everyone?

Even if you trust everyone to try, do you trust them to not fuck up?

Because that's the problem, isn't it?

Given brains fundamentally don't work, even with the help of photos that fundamentally don't work either, how the fuck is history supposed to work?

Does that get you down like it does me?

Rasputin

B, M, *and* P *are all dressed as Rasputin, with varying degrees of excellence.* B *should have the most realistic and beautiful beard.*

P (*listening*). Mm hmm.

B (*listening*). Mm hmm.

M (*listening*). Mm hmm.

P. In food or – [*Drink, the poison.*] ?

B (*listening*). Mm hmm.

M (*listening*). Mm hmm.

P. Cool.

B. Am I getting actual, [*food*] or just – ?

M (*listening*). Mm hmm.

P (*listening*). Mm hmm.

B. And I realise – [*that he's poisoned me*] ?

M. And are we friends or – [*am I suspicious of him*] ?

P (*listening*). Mm hmm.

B (*listening*). Mm hmm.

M. Ohhhh, interesting [*that this isn't necessarily what really happened*] !

P. But this isn't what actually – [*happened*] ?

B (*listening*). Mm hmm.

M (*listening*). Mm hmm.

P. Yeah, because I thought I remembered – [*him dying some other way*] ?

B. And is he – [*Prince Yusupov, where is he standing relative to Rasputin?*] ?

M (*listening*). Mm hmm.

P (*listening*). Mm hmm.

B. And do I say anything to him or – [*not*] ?

M (*listening*). Mm hmm.

P (*listening*). Mm hmm.

B. Cool.

M. Is it cool if I try out a kind of twitchy, you know, nerve – [*damage*] ?

P (*listening*). Mm hmm.

B (*listening*). Mm hmm.

M. Cool.

They all eat poisoned food and die extravagantly. After a
moment, they recover and look out through the audience for
approval.

P. Yeah? [*That okay?*]

B. Yeah?

M. Yeah?

P (*listening*). Mm hmm.

B (*listening*). Mm hmm.

M (*listening*). Mm hmm.

P. In the – [*head*] ?

B (*listening*). Mm hmm.

M (*listening*). Mm hmm.

P. Cool.

B. So, just bend and then – [*get shot*] ?

M (*listening*). Mm hmm.

P (*listening*). Mm hmm.

B. Through here? (*The chest.*)

M. And do I die or – [*not yet*] ?

P (*listening*). Mm hmm.

B (*listening*). Mm hmm.

M. Cool, because I was pretty sure that he – [*didn't die from that*]

P. So, this isn't what actually – [*happened*] ?

B (*listening*). Mm hmm.

M (*listening*). Mm hmm.

P. Yeah, duhDOI! Sorry, cool. [*That was a stupid question.*]

B. Obviously, given we just – [*showed him dying of poison.*]

M (*listening*). Mm hmm.

P (*listening*). Mm hmm.

B. Fast or – [*slow, death*] ?

M (*listening*). Mm hmm.

P (*listening*). Mm hmm.

B. Cool.

M. Is it cool if I try out a kind of twitchy, you know, nerve –
[*damage*] ?

P (*listening*). Mm hmm.

B (*listening*). Mm hmm.

M. Cool.

> *They get shot in the head and die extravagantly. After a moment
> they recover and look out through the audience for approval.*

P. Yeah?

B. Yeah?

M. Yeah?

P (*listening*). Mm hmm.

B (*listening*). Mm hmm.

M (*listening*). Mm hmm.

P. So, under – [*ice.*]

B (*listening*). Mm hmm.

M (*listening*). Mm hmm.

P. Cool.

B. Could I not just – [*break it*] ?

M (*listening*). Mm hmm.

P (*listening*). Mm hmm.

B. Yeah, fair. [*Russian winter equals thick ice.*]

M. And am I panicked or – [*fatigued*] ?

P (*listening*). Mm hmm.

B (*listening*). Mm hmm.

M. Cool. So, first – [*one and then the other*]

P. And is this where he – [*actually died*] ?

B (*listening*). Mm hmm.

M (*listening*). Mm hmm.

P. Oooooh freaky [*that it's disputed still*] !

B. Because then wasn't it when they set him on fire – [*that he sat up*] ?

M (*listening*). Mm hmm.

P (*listening*). Mm hmm.

B. Oh, right, tendons, okay. Didn't know that. [*That uncut tendons tighten when burned.*]

M (*listening*). Mm hmm.

P (*listening*). Mm hmm.

B. Cool.

M. Is it cool if I try out a kind of twitchy, you know, nerve – [*damage*] ?

P (*listening*). Mm hmm.

B (*listening*). Mm hmm.

M. Cool.

> *They drown under the ice of a Russian river and die extravagantly. After a moment they recover, and look out through the audience for approval.*

P. Yeah?

B. Yeah?

M. Yeah?

P. Thanks.

B. It's been a real… [*honour.*]

M. Cool.

P. Cool.

B. Cool.

M. Cool.

The casting is over. The auditionees take a break, grab a coffee, maybe air out their scalps and faces from under their beards/ wigs. There's a moment where it would be weirder for them not to look at each other, and then having looked at each other it would be weirder to say nothing than to say anything.

P. Phew!

B. Phew!

M. Yeah.

P. I love this – (B*'s robe*.) the fabric, where did you get it?

B. Oh, thanks, I just have aunts.

M. In-your-house ants?

P. No, like someone's sisters.

B. AWNTS.

M. Ohhhh.

P. A parent.

B. Who I got this off.

M. Right.

P. Yeah.

B. Rasputin!

M. The way you do!

P. I'm kind of loving it.

B. Rasputeen?

M. I mean I'm not Russian.

P. Raspyewtin?

B. What's Mark like?!

M. Do you know him?

P. I think he's great.

B. We were in college together.

M. So, you're not an actor?

P. A real sensibility.

B. He just likes my face, he asked me to come along but I'm really out of my depth here.

M. He's doing so well!

P. Yeah, like, fayMOOSH.

B. All of a sudden!

M. Is that weird?

P. Are you staying friends?

B. Trying, anyway. He's so busy, in demand.

M. Since he did that music video for those guys?

P. Who are just exploding everywhere, America – !

B. America! (*Not in unison with* P.)

M. Guess we know who's getting the part!

P. Inside track!

B. I'm really out of my depth here.

M. Just like Rasputin! Because he drowned?

P. Was he not dead going into the river?

B. Or didn't he live until he was on fire?

M. When was he on fire?

P. Before or after he was poisoned?

B. Poisoned, shot, ran away, shot again, drowned, burned, and it LOOKED like he was still alive because the heat made his tendons contract.

M. You really know Rasputin.

P. Was he in college with you and Mark?!

B. Year below until he dropped out!

M. I heard he had mental health.

P. So much mental health.

B. I mean he did get poisoned, shot, shot again, drowned, and burned that one time.

M. And all he did was start the Russian Revolution. Did he do that?

P. I mean, he was there – ?

B. Died the December before, I think? [*This is right.*]

M. I'm not going to lie, everything I know about Rasputin is from the film.

P. Where he's an undead sorcerer with a Romanian batfriend?

B. In fairness, in the film he does start the Russian Revolution.

M. With green ghosts.

P. Were they there?

B. If they're a metaphor for striking factory workers, then yeah?!

M. Are you a bit of a nerd?

P. I think you're a bit of a nerd.

B. I'm not, I just have the internet.

M. Do you know everything?

P. How much do you know?

B. Not everything, like, five?

M. Wow.

P. Wow.

B. I looked it up when Mark asked me to come along to this, not that historical accuracy is a big thing if his Rasputin dies a shitload of ways or might be a woman.

M. Or in music videos generally.

P. I know something!

B. Yeah?

M. Yeah?

P. About Rasputin!

B. Yeah?

M (*offering a grape from a snack table*). Grape?

P. The reason that films have to say that thing, you know, This is a work of fiction, any resemblance to, to –

B. Persons living or dead?

M. Living or dead! (*Not in unison with* B.)

P. That, yeah! The reasons films have to say that is because the guy who killed Rasputin sued the makers of the film for implying Rasputin raped his wife.

B. What?!

M. Wow.

P. In maybe the sixties or something?

B. That's amazing.

M. Not in the cartoon with the Romanian batfriend and the green ghosts?

P. Different film.

B. Prince Yusupov.

M. I was thinking I didn't remember that.

P. Who?

B. His name, Prince Yusupov.

M. I don't know anything about Rasputin, except he was the lover of the Russian Queen.

P. Tsarina. I know that.

B. Are you saying that because of Boney M, though?

M. No…

P. Is that true, though?

B. I don't know.

M. Boney M wouldn't lie to us.

P. They weren't even alive when Babylon, though.

B. True.

M. I feel really ignorant.

P. In fairness though, why should you know about Rasputin, though?

B. He wasn't objectively important.

M. Yeah, but if he's not I should probably just not know anything at all about him, if he's not important at all then I shouldn't think he started the Russian Revolution with green ghosts.

P. Yeah, but also, it's not like he's, I don't know, Hitler.

B. I don't know, have you ever seen the two of them in the same room?

M. I haven't. Fuck.

P. Fuck, me neither.

B. Proof.

M. I do know things about Hitler.

P. He was an artist.

B. Vegetarian.

M. And he was in a beer hall one time.

P. I know that, too.

B. And me.

M. But I don't know why.

P. Neither do I.

B. Nope.

M. Or anything about Pol Pot.

P. I want to say Cambodia – ?

B. Khmer Rouge, yeah.

M. THAT'S how you say that.

P. I always wondered.

B. No one knows everything.

M. And who the fuck is Charlemagne?

P. Actually, yeah?

B. No idea.

M. So, like, why Rasputin fucked the Queen a hundred years ago is the least of my worries.

P. Tsarina.

B. Pretty much exactly, weird, one hundred years ago, if he did. Fuck her.

M. You're the nerd, is he important at all or should I skip him and go straight to Charlemagne?

P. Yeah, nerd.

B. I'm really not a nerd.

M. You're a relative nerd.

P. Yeah, nerd.

B. I don't know if he's important.

M. OH!

P. Oh?

B. Oh?

M. I know something!

P. Yeah?

B. Yeah?

M. Maybe he's important because of South Korea?

P. Yeah?

B. Yeah?

M. Choi Soon Sil? (*Truly mangling the pronunciation and knowing it.*)

P. Yeah?

B. Yeah?

M. A couple of years ago?

P. All I know about South Korea is that it's the good Korea.

B. Your faith is touching.

M. They impeached their president because she was taking advice on really big issues from this kooky spiritualist advisor? Basically exactly like how Rasputin pissed off Russia by influencing the Tsarina when she was vulnerable because her son was sick? That happened, right?

P. Yeah?

B. Yeah.

M. Something something history, doomed to repeat itself. Something something, rulers, religion, church, state, babies, septic tanks, I can't believe I know something!

P. YOU'RE the nerd!

B. YES.

M. I'm just a Libra.

P (*to* B). I'm sorry for your crown.

B. I was never a nerd. Mark just brought it up and I just interneted it. Because the song is called 'Echo', because people kind of do after they're dead, they echo, and like echoes they kind of distort and become unrecognisable over enough time. Which is why he's filming all of the different deaths people think Rasputin died, and probably him fucking and not fucking and healing and not healing the Tsarina and her son, respectively. And why it's Rasputin at all, because he's an echo who was never a sound in the first place.

M. Whoa, poet.

P. Did Mark come up with that?

B. No, I did, because I love the idea even if I think Mark is a creep who groped me while asking me to be in this video.

M. Oh my god.

P. Shit, I'm sorry to hear that.

B. I didn't really say that.

M. Whoa, poet.

P. Mark is so incredible.

B. He is. I said that.

We don't know why we know Rasputin is a bad guy. Because knowing would mean knowing all of Russian history.

M. Which is, like, five.

P. At least five.

B. So we don't, we just keep saying what's been said until it becomes true. Did you know Rasputin had kids?

M. No!

P. No!

B. Seven! But lots of them died. But he had a daughter, Maria, who lived. And after her dad was killed, she ended up working in a CIRCUS where her act was to RE-ENACT PRINCE YUSUPOV

KILLING HER FATHER, because that was what people wanted. To see the daughter of the mad monk, who wasn't actually mad or a monk, acting out his death. Because they hated him. They believed he was this cartoon villain, seventy years before the cartoon with his Romanian batfriend even came out. They wanted to see him shot, even if he wasn't shot, because he should have been shot.

And she needed money because she needed to eat, so she had to do the act even though she hated it, because she knew that the world wouldn't let her remember her father any way but that way.

She said once that every night as she shot him she felt a pang of sorrow, even though it wasn't him, even though it wasn't real, but if you tell that story enough, it has to start to feel true. And then one night you face your father across the stage, you shoot him, and it's easy.

A WOMAN, *an imperious and spooky woman, a tsarina of a woman, with a face made of jewels, shoots* B. B *falls dead.* M *and* P *look at the body, then at the* TSARINA/MARIA FIGURE, *and try to run. There are anothe two shots and they fall dead. The* TSARINA/MARIA *regards the audience impassively. The stage is flooded with* RASPUTINS *whose faces are obscured by their enormous seventies hair. They all die as a distorted version of Boney M's 'Ra Ra Rasputin' plays.*

Zoom Out

If your voice-over aged over the course of the show, at this point it should reprise its ageing from youngest to oldest all over again.

In five minutes you'll remember this as the complicated bit you didn't understand.

You'll remember the word Eigenface because it sounds like the name of a cool American boy, Randy Eigenface.

You know, Randy Eigenface who's taking Mandy

Spoopelpeim to the Sadie Hawkin's dance?

In five hours, in a club, talking to the friend you're sitting beside right now, you'll misremember Mandy's second name as Poopelspeim. Your friend won't remark on it, so you'll continue to remember it as Poopelspeim.

You will also have no idea what an actual eigenface is, even though I explained.

In five days you'll remember you were asked to raise your hand in answer to questions, but will have no memory of what those questions were.

In five weeks, you'll remember that there was music here, but not what it sounded like. You'll think of it as having been pale green and curvilinear. Why, I don't know, but those are the clues your brain will leave you with.

In five months, you'll pass James in the street and not know who he is. You'll think maybe you should, for some reason, and you'll think he has a fatherly vibe, like maybe you'd like to have a child with him. Or two. Which is bizarre. You don't want kids, at ALL, let alone TWO. Gas.

In five years, you will look strange to yourself in the photo you took in the club with your friend after this show. You won't remember why you were out together, or what you spoke about. You'll just think Oh GOD, my HAIR.

In five decades, you will be old, if not dead, and your children – if you have any's – photos of you will predominantly represent you as an old person, even though you were only old that one time. Style will have looped back around so that, if they ever see the photo you take later tonight with your friend in the club, they'll be surprised by how cool your hair is.

At this point, the voice-over drops out, leaving silent projected text on its own.

In five centuries, no digital photos of you will remain because digital technology is no longer used, either because a utopic society has outgrown it, or because a dystopic society has lost it. Analogue photos of you still exist in museums and archives of such technology. The fact that you are in them has nothing to do with their preservation. Your hairstyle is hilarious to the enlightened or degraded youth of the twenty-sixth century.

In five millennia, Earth will receive intelligent communication in the form of a perfect sphere of an unknown material whose emission spectrum's bands are in a ratio of 2 to the sum of the first two primes (5) to the sum of that many sums of primes (62) to the sum of that many sums of sums of primes (2,452,441) and so on. No intelligent life will remain to appreciate this recursive harmony. We're long gone. It just gives some badgers cancer.

Music should come to a gradual imperceptible halt in time for the ending.

In five billennia, for reasons not tractable to current science, time has stopped, for lack of a better less chronocentric word. In this new unplace that has always been, nothing becomes. The past no longer echoes. Silence falls. What a relief.

The End.

BEFORE YOU SAY ANYTHING

Carys D. Coburn
with MALAPROP THEATRE

Introduction

Before You Say Anything was made under lockdown conditions. We got a call from Ruth at the Dublin Fringe Festival to ask us if we would be interested in making a show as part of a necessarily small programme, for a necessarily small audience. We said yes. It was the spring/summer of 2020 – there was a lot happening in the world that demanded some kind of response, some kind of deeper thinking through, but we knew we didn't want to perform the headlines. There are obvious reasons for us to be talking about public health and policing: the pandemic and the global protests following the murder of George Floyd respectively. As we talked, we moved away from their most recent collision – the violent suppression of protests in the name of Covid-safety – and towards their historical intertwining, how health measures have invariably facilitated the violent policing of the already overpoliced.

We found ourselves talking about the long shadow of nineteenth-century sus laws. You could go back as far as the Georgian Vagrancy Act of 1824; or you could pick up from the Victorian Offences Against the Person Act of 1861, Contagious Diseases Act of 1864, or the 1885 Criminal Law Amendment Act modifying the act of '61. The last of these might seem prescient, a law criminalising 'gross indecency' between men just a few years before the police discover a male brothel in Cleveland Street frequented by some very posh clients. (ALLEGEDLY.)

But it only looks prescient if you ignore the distinctively Irish chapter of the story from 1884, the year before the law. Which, of course, we refuse to do. Before Cleveland Street there was Dublin Castle: Anglo-Irish soldiers accused of having gay orgies! Shocking! In the seat (oh my) of the colonial government! Who'd want to ignore that?

A series of laws aimed at combatting crime or disease by combatting prostitution or buggery by giving the police the power to stop and search on the basis of suspicion. And we know who the police like to suspect: the poor, the queer, the mad, the melanated. Maybe it shouldn't be a surprise that they were still at it a hundred years later in Toxteth and Brixton. Amongst other places – the year after Black youth rose up, said *NO MORE,* the English Collective of Prostitutes did the same and occupied a church in King's Cross to protest their treatment by the police – as detailed in Selma James' essay *Hookers in the House of the Lord.*

A disease that you catch in a hospital is *iatrogenic.* Should we borrow it as the name for violence brought about by people claiming to prevent it? Or is there a word for that already? (Is that word just policing?)

It was at this point that the Fringe got in touch with an either/or choice for us: would we rather present our piece in a retail unit, or in the Chapel Royal in Dublin Castle? This felt fated, a little spooky even. How could we say no to the chance to stage the inquiry on the site of the history?

And so. The show we ended up making is a trio of variations on the theme of police and churches and public nudity. The Chapel Royal in the 1880s, as a gay man flees the scene of a fuck gone wrong; a London church in the 1980s, as a young Irish woman flees a marriage gone wrong; an Irish church in the present day, as a woman buries her sister. All the footnotes are in there somewhere. It was a small show so the citations had to be oblique, in passing, incidental to the action we were able to pull off under the circumstances. But see if you can spot them.

Finally: *Before You Say Anything* was dedicated to the memory of Dara Quigley, with the permission of her family. Her case is an unmistakeable precedent if you want to talk about the Gardaí and image-based abuse, how their handling of it can compound the initial wrong even in those cases where they are not themselves the perpetrators. We felt the respectful thing to do was acknowledge that.

Before You Say Anything was first performed at the Chapel Royal in Dublin Castle on 5 September 2020, as part of Dublin Fringe Festival 2020: Pilot Light Edition. The cast was as follows:

G	Ghaliah Conroy
M	Maeve O'Mahony
P	Peter Corboy
Writer	Carys D. Coburn
	with MALAPROP
Director	Claire O'Reilly
Stage Manager and	
Assistant Director	Ursula McGinn
Costume and Set Design	Molly O'Cathain
Composer	Jennifer O'Malley
Lighting Design	Suzie Cummins
Producer	Carla Rogers

A co-commission from Dublin Fringe Festival and the Abbey Theatre.

Supported by the Office of Public Works (OPW) and Dublin Castle. Developed at FRINGE LAB with the support of Dublin Fringe Festival.

Characters

G
M
P

Note on the Dialogue

A dash (–) at the end of a line indicates an interruption from the
next speaker.

A slash (/) indicates overlapping dialogue.

Sorbet One

'Sorbet' is a MALAPROP shorthand for a section where plot isn't in the foreground. In application speak, we sometimes call them 'abstract flourishes', moments whose meaning is up for grabs, non-verbal, retroactively reinterpreted in light of what happens later.

This type of fauxbatim text, auto-interruptive and disfluent, might be sung, or half-sung, psalmodised or recited, or otherwise heightened; it's marked throughout with curly brackets. In our production, M entered slowly in her black funeral clothes for the third and final section of the show while singing this text as a kind of funeral march chorale. P and G were singing with her from the choir balconies.

M. {In my head there's a universe

It keeps going around in my head that somewhere

You didn't do what you did and she's alive

And I don't get to live there because you did do what you did}

The Eighteen Eighties

The Chapel Royal itself. P runs in naked holding his late nineteenth-century clothes. He finds a spot which is less totally exposed, and begins to dress. As he dresses, he speaks.

P. So before you say anything, I know some of you might be family.

Which just adds verisimilitude, duckies.

Because you never know who you'll see.

Which is part of the appeal.

The looking around, the having a nose, the squeezing the peaches to see if they're firm.

Or mouldy.

Or if your thumb goes right into it, oops, didn't mean to do that, now I'm all gooey.

So look around at each other.

Decide who you'd fuck.

Decide who you'll fuck if they take you somewhere and buy you a drink first, who you'll let buy you a drink but won't fuck, *I've just remembered I'm meeting a friend,* who you won't drink with but might fuck, who you'll talk to but won't fuck, who you'll fuck but won't talk to.

A suggestion that P *is categorising the audience for himself as he outlines the categories.*

Family excluded, of course, we're deviants but there's such a thing as taste.

Picks someone.

Though if you were my brother –

I'm codding, I wouldn't fuck you.

Wouldn't want you to fall pregnant.

Frigging only.

But if they're family, you just decide if you'll peach on them to Grandmother at Christmas before they have a chance to peach on you.

The jewels are glass but you still want to inherit.

And if you say cousin Daniel is a bugger before he says you're one, who's going to believe a bugger?

Because sometimes the only way to win is not to fight.

And sometimes the only way not to fight is to hit them hard when they've done nothing.

So look around at each other.

Decide who you'd name to the long strong arm of *la loi.*

Because if they burst in and grab you, you will name someone.

No one too rich, because bribes.

No one too poor, because Christian Charity.

Not the brutes, because *a big thing like him? Darling you're having me on.*

And not the queeniest queens, because the constables hurt them
enough already.

Maybe you. (*Pick someone.*)

You'd satisfy them.

But it's a shame.

You're my sort.

Not too big, not too small, not too hot, not too cold.

I'm not a blond, and you're not a bear, but you're just right.

I had one a bit like you, a while back.

And he takes me back to his castle.

It's really a castle, cross my desiccated.

He's government, debauching the Native.

*If you're not in a post-colonial context and 'Native' doesn't
fit, you can replace it with a campy word like Rustic/Swain/
Proletarian.*

Shuts the bedroom door and gets me up against it.

Not rough, just strong, and then very still, barely moving.

And takes my hand and puts it on his stomach, and slides it
down, and just holds it there.

Holding me holding him.

And he's not even hard yet but it's nice, warm and solid and just,
alive? Interested?

And we're breathing into each other's mouths, his face is that
close to mine, but not doing anything, and hard to say what he's
looking at because it's not my eyes but it's me, because it'd have
to be, it's that close.

And then he kisses me, very slowly, here, my lower lip with
both of his, and then both of mine with both of his, a kiss I'd
lean into but he's holding my neck.

And I can feel him getting hard in my hand as we kiss.

And feeling that I'm getting [hard] –

I want him to touch me back, but I don't want him to stop doing
anything he's doing.

One of those where you wish, you nearly think, if you stayed like this you'd both come off, and the only reason you don't is because you lose patience and get started on all the other things.

Which is what happened then.

We committed all the unspeakable acts, all five of them.

(*Pick someone*.) If you're counting and coming up short, hang around after the show.

And I go to clean up, wipe the windows, polish the knob, sluice the flue, and I push on the door to the loo but it hits something and stops halfway, and I see that there's two men in there looking at me.

And maybe they're his friends who've been having themselves some fun too, and he just never mentioned.

But maybe they're constables.

Or maybe they want to kill me.

Or all three.

And I'm thinking about a few years back when they cleared all the gay girls out of Bull Lane, because they were giving soldiers the pox or that's the story, and the state of them when they came out the wagon.

Story goes that Kitty Small sits on the table, puts her legs up, and the doctor faints.

They weren't all on the street before, but they were after.

I'm thinking about the state of the postboys who aren't sly enough with their come-ons.

Or the ones who're that pretty that no one believes they're not selling it, even when they're not, because they'd be stupid not to.

For a while, for a while they're that pretty.

And that's the ones who come back.

Don't know what happened to him that you always saw in the facilities, or him that wore the wigs, or the girl who barbered for all them with the short hair, or the one I had at the theatre who gave me his hankie for my hand, or the one who was HUGE, or the one who was HAIRY – (*Using real audience members*.) or the one that looked like you, or like you, or like you.

Your newspaper man will say it's about – (*Quoting*.) curbing unhealthy and criminal tendencies.

But it wouldn't be criminal if they just changed the law.

And it wouldn't be unhealthy if they didn't do you five in a row.

But I see those men and I'm out the door before I know it.

And I'm not dressed, but when I think I might go back I hear someone running after me.

So I start running, and I'm down the stairs, and I turn without looking, and then I turn again, again without looking, and I can't find the road, but I see a door and I go through.

And it's dark, but I can tell it's a big room.

And I knock something, and something in the room – [Vibrates? Resonates? Chimes?]

Sound design builds.

And I realise it's an organ, there's an organ, and I realise this is a chapel.

And I've always been musical.

He sings us into the next section.

Sorbet Two

M. {It is unclear if the Garda concerned has returned to work or
   And with regards to prosecution or disciplinary action
   Regretfully cannot comment on ongoing internal inquiries}

The Nineteen Eighties

A London church. G runs in naked and finds a less exposed spot to hunker down in.

P, wearing a priest's cassock, enters and spots G.

G. C'mere, before you say anything, just [know] –

Take a second and think that I know, okay?

P. Okay.

G. Do you have a phone I can use?

P. Here?

G. Yes here.

P. Yes.

G. And do you have anything I can wear?

P. I – [don't]

Actually, there's some things that were left in / during the week.

G. Are you Irish? /

P. For me to give away, which I suppose is what I'd be [doing] – and yes! Yes I am.

G. Me too.

P. There you are then.

G. What?

P. I don't know either.

–

I've never met – [a Black Irish person before.]

G. What?

P. Doesn't matter.

G. Clothes?

P. Right. One sec.

P goes and finds a box of clothes, which he goes to hand to G, and then tries to slide to her from a distance. G is not so much shy as wary in how she moves around P *as she starts to get clothes from the box.* M *starts to sing from offstage, maybe something that starts off as a brisk warm-up and gradually becomes more of a expressive vocalise.*

Margaret's doing singing lessons at eight. So we're not alone!

G. Okay?

P. If you felt uneasy, just, being alone with me.

G. No?

P. –

Thought this might be a takeover, myself, when I saw you!

G. What?

P. Just there was that thing a whileen back, King's Cross, a bunch of working girls went in for an evening service and refused to leave. Protest. Police have been throwing their weight around, harassing them. Very clever, actually, very theatrical, black masks to hide their identities, like the Spirit or the Phantom if you ever read them, or listened, but very clever to draw attention to the problem, make them cop on to themselves, / remind them they know better.

G. Working girls? /

P. The police I meant, but I don't know why I said that. Old-fashioned moment. Prostitutes. I mean prostitutes. They were very nice, some of my friends were helping out, babysat their kids and brought them food, big things of curry mostly, everything had to be vegetarian. Don't know why.

G. Probably because they were all vegetarian.

P. Right.

G. Do you think I'm a prostitute?

P. –

No?

G. Because I'm not.

P. Right.

Just –

G. Yeah?

P. Given – [nudity.]

G. But if I was a prozzy then me being walking around naked is like – [giving it away]?

Don't know about you, but my butcher doesn't stand in the street fucking hearts and tongues at traffic.

P. That's a point.

G. Cow hearts and tongues like.

P. Yeah.

–

It wouldn't be for me to judge, is all I'd say more.

G. Which?

P. If you were, I mean.

G. A prostitute?

P. I know lots of young people come to London because they're sick of the parish the parish the parish – (*Trying to be knowing.*) that the church isn't 'cool', and I can understand that.

G. Can you?

P. Yes, yes I can, We talk a lot about the grace of God but we haven't always been graceful. And I want that to change. Things need to.

G. Yeah?

P. I think, I think that's important.

G. That's nice and all, but I amn't a prostitute.

P. Right.

G. My husband tried to kill me.

P. –

Right.

G. Yeah.

P. Have you – ?

G. Yeah?

P. Or, do you want to call the police?

G. On my husband?

P. You know best, I'm sure, if this is something that'll blow over, sort itself out, or if –

G. Ask me what he does.

P. Your husband?

G. What do you think he does, yeah. Have a guess.

P. –

He's police?

G. A detective. Very proud of that. Young for it.

P. And do you need – [medical attention]?

G. Yeah?

P. Just I didn't see any bruises, or injuries I should say, but – [you might have some.]

G. No.

P. Oh. (*Unsure*.) That's good?

G. Should have waited around, should I?

P. No.

–

I have a wig if you want?

G. A wig?

P. Just if you want, though it's blonde.

G. Who gave you that?

P. That is a question which is very, it's actually mine.

G. Your wig?

P. For singalongs.

–

We have little piano parties, showtunes and standards mostly, dress up is just sometimes to be gas, me and some of the other – [priests? Gays?]

G. I'm not in disguise.

P. Right.

G. I just need clothes.

P. Of course.

G. And I'm really not a blonde.

P. There is that.

G. But cheers. Phone?

P. In the office, around the back. (G *moves off in the direction indicated,* P*'s next line out to audience:*)

I hear her say –

G *dances around these lines.* M*'s music becomes less sparse, more present, more.*

G. Just ran and ran and ran

Much worse

Whenever before it was always

If it's to hand, or if I fall

But I came down from the shower and he's sitting there and there's a hammer on the table

So I know that this time it's not just

Snap or split or

That it's not going to be sorry I didn't mean it

He's gone out to the shed just to get it like

Thought about it and decided

Saying I'm leaving him

Saying I can't hurt him like this

Ripped the towel off me but I got away

The dance ebbs, and so does the music.

P. All done?

G. Thanks. She's picking me up, half an hour or so.

P. You can keep the clothes.

G. I can bring them back?

P. Please.

G. I don't want them.

P. Then I'll be happy to take them.

–

How old are you?

G. Twenty-two.

P. Young enough to be married.

G. You're young enough to be a priest.

P. You think?

G. And if this is a rude question, tell me to fuck off –

P. I'm gay.

G. Why?

P. Am I gay?

G. Are you a priest?

P. –

I wanted grace. There's things we can't deserve until we've already been given them. And there's things we can't get given until we've given them away. So I wanted to give.

G. Like?

P. Like?

G. Like what things?

P. Love. Acceptance. Kindness, even. Why'd you marry him?

G. Because I asked him and he said yes.

P. And why'd you ask him?

G. Because he was going to ask me, and if I said no he would've killed me.

Phone rings.

P. Is that – ?

G. My friend?

P. Does she have the number?

G. No.

> P *goes and picks up the phone. G dances, the rhythms of the dance interlocking with the rhythms of* P's *responses. The music swells again.*

> I hear him say –

P. Yes?

> No.

> No.

> Yes.

> Yes.

> Yes.

> Yes.

> I wouldn't use that language but

> Well *as* an officer of the law you should

> Half-caste, or, light-skinned anyway but

> No, she's married, she's just having a bit of

> Right.

> Right.

> Yes.

> Yes.

> No.

> *The dance and music ebbs.*

G. Police?

P. Yes.

G. Looking for me?

P. Yes, or, there's been a report of a woman soliciting outside the church. They're on their way down now.

G. So yes. He must have followed me, rung it in from a box.

P. But I told them that you aren't – [a prostitute.]

G. Doesn't matter.

P. That you haven't done anything, or weren't going to even.

G. Definitely not if they arrest me!

P. Why would he do that?

G. Teach me a lesson probably.

P. But his own wife?

G. –

You said your friends were helping?

P. With the protest?

G. But not you, no? You didn't make any vegetarian curry?

P. No.

G. That friends from the church? Never thought about that, do priests all get together, sink a rake of pints? Play bridge? Go for fish and chips after Friday-night mass?

P. No.

G. No they don't?

P. No it's not friends from the church, it's friends from, from meetings. Political meetings, discussions. About the movement. And I didn't make any curry because, maybe I should have, but I see my role as offering guidance when people feel lost. So when I've dealt with, or talked to, prostitutes, that was when. Do you think that's wrong?

G. Just you sound so shocked by everything I say, and I don't believe it. I don't believe you're that shocked, your church is here, neighbourhood like this, only way you're that shocked is if you never talk to anyone.

P. –

Not never, but maybe I'm not doing enough.

G. 'People who feel lost', you said.

P. Yes?

G. That make you feel special? You're the one who can tell people what's wrong with them?

P. I wouldn't say that.

G. What would you say? /

P. That there's something wrong with you. I don't know, I'd say that people need to see properly before they can act properly, and that's what I'm good at.

G. You like it better when the problem isn't obvious, sounds like. Because when it's obvious it's obvious what you should do, you don't have to be wise or clever or, they're the same, but you don't have to be anything. You just have to do something. Something anyone could do, but no one wants to do it.

P. –

I'll talk to them for you when they get here if you want.

G. The police?

P. If they're from the local station they'll know me.

G. Tell them no worries, not a prozzy, just naked and Black?

P. You're not naked any more.

G. Yeah. Thanks.

P. I could even, sort of, distract them?

G. While I Do A Getaway?

P. I suppose.

G. To where?

P. –

You don't have family here?

G. Ma's in prison, sister's pregnant and lost the last one, don't want to land on her with all this in case she loses this one. The stress like, door kicked in and all that.

P. –

And if I can ask – [what about your dad?]

G. Won't talk to me because I married police.

P. Right.

G. Know what you can do?

P. Yes?

G. See if he's outside? White man, thirties, dark hair, moustache. Blue eyes, but maybe don't get that close. In a green Ford.

P. What kind?

G. Of Ford?

P. Yes.

G. Cortina.

P. –

I don't actually know cars.

G. The car everyone has.

P. Right. And you'll be okay?

G. Okay?

P. Here on your own if I – [go outside.]

G. Yeah. I'm fine on my own.

P *goes.*

Sorbet Three

M. {Preventative is one word another is
What I want to know is
What I want you to tell me if you can is
What did you prevent?
Because they never get a chance to do it did they?
So we never get to know do we?}

The Twenty Teens

An Irish church.

M. {Before you say anything

We've heard enough about her death

So I'll talk about her what she was like and that's all}

P. I know some of you might be family, which might be awkward, or might be exactly what you need.

Because we're talking about the worst moment of your life.

So look around at each other.

Decide who you'd want to see when you're more scared than you've ever been.

G. Bearing in mind you're naked, which is a factor, but probably not the actual problem.

M. {We've heard enough about her death

So I'll talk about her what she was like and that's all

When you're kids it's all just how people are

They like this they don't like that

And she didn't like or

She hated, more like, she hated having her hair cut

Screaming crying she'd be, making a show of us

So Ma always did that for her

And for years that was all it ever was

It was times she was confused

Only person ever she was a risk to was herself}

P. That's what her sister says in the video from before she was sick of journalists.

G. Her sister didn't have to become a social worker afterwards because she was one already.

Her ma's in literacy.

P. Her brother's in addiction, in the good way, not the bad way, but it used to be the bad way, which is why he's so good at being at it in the good way.

G. They try to talk calmly to their groups about her but cry.

P. She wanted to be a photographer.

M. {She was a photographer}

G. If you've to wait until they pay you to call yourself an artist then no one is.

P. They grew up in a neighbourhood on fire.

    Where everyone who gets out goes back in for everyone still stuck.

G. Because they know that the past doesn't stop burning just because you've left it.

P. Because they breathed it in, so it's too late to just live.

G. Because if it's too late for you, save someone else before it's too late for them.

    G's dancing starts to take off.

M. {I never believed in jails even before

    But this has been a test a real test of but all in all

    I don't want a sentence I want to look him in his face

    I want to ask him why you have a woman in a cell

    A naked woman in a cell and your instinct your first response

    How do you justify taking pictures to yourself even

    That's my question}

G. When the audio is released everyone hears that the emergency call says

P. There's a woman here, walking down the street, she's very upset and she's not got much on but she's just walking down the street

M. {Preventative custody okay but the law says

    You take someone in, a doctor sees them

    Where's the call to the doctor?}

P. She ran away when she was fifteen, and two days later when she was brought home crying in a Garda car she said

G. I didn't want to go but it was too hard to stay

M. {Time to take photos of her time to send them

    No time to call a doctor like the law says explain that}

P. Aged fifteen she kept crying and kept saying

G. They wouldn't bring me home until I let them take my fingerprints, they took my shoes my belt and searched me the two of them two men one just watching, and then they say we

have to ask, and I say no, no fingerprints, and then I was all
night in a box in my bare feet until I said yes until I let them,
they've got them now, and I know you don't believe me but they
wouldn't bring me home

M. {They'll say preventative and that sounds official

But we know what preventative means at this point don't we

Preventative means arresting people who've done fuck-all}

P. She didn't leave a note

But maybe she felt she had no time to write one

The dance hits a wall, to be resumed shortly.

M. You've some fucking nerve

P. Is what her sister says to the two Gardaí who come to the funeral.

G. Though not immediately because she spots them when the little
cousins are bringing up the offerings.

G. Framed photo of her aged nine in her – (*Say 'Gah' not 'Jee Ay
Ay'.*) GAA gear.

P. Framed photo she took aged twenty down the Blackpitts, just
after she moved up to Dublin, little girl on a sixteen-hand horse.

G. The three Stinger bars they had to order from Amazon hating
themselves, because the Mace that used to be the cornershop
doesn't do her favourites any more.

M. You've some fucking nerve.

G. We're just here to pay our respects / on behalf of the station.

M. Came specially did you?

G. Sorry?

M. Middle of the day, you're in uniform, did you get a call about
something in the town, not your spot but you're just that good,
care that much, you come to check it out and just decide to drop
in for the funeral, or did you drive down specially for this?

G. We came for the funeral.

M. You on the clock, are you? Getting paid to be here?

G. We wanted to say how sorry we are / that the answers you
deserve are taking so long to get to you –

M. I should fucking hope you're sorry, you fucking should be,
my ma's over there, my ma is up the front shaking hands with
everyone and thanking them while she's wondering, while she's
having to think Have They Seen Those Photos Of Her, Is That
What They Have In Their Head, Is That How She's Going To Be
Remembered, and don't give me any of that On Behalf of The
Station because I know exactly who you are Mr Fucking Man /
walking in here today like nothing can touch you but it's going
to –

P. I – /

G. Don't – /

M. We'll have your fucking badge, that's your face clear as
anything in the video, that's you grabbing her by her fucking
hair, proud of that, are you? Sick woman, lost, confused,
screaming crying, / all you can think to do is reef her into the
back of a car? Been talking to that couple who were there and
all, lovely people, they said you didn't even try and talk to her,
small danger you'd find out she lived two minutes around the
fucking corner, could have brought her home, made her a cup
of tea, she'd be alive today, or are you going to try and tell me
that's nothing to do with anything? She would have done it even
if you hadn't picked her up again, fucked her in a cell again, put
her out of her mind remembering all the other times when she's
already struggling? Because say it to my face if that's what it's
going to be in the papers, and it's going to be in the papers, you
can be sure of that, this is not disappearing, but if that's what
it's going to be then try and tell me to my face she didn't die
because one of you cunts took photos of the mad bitch in the cell
and put them out there for everyone forever.

G. –

I think it might be best if we left, and we regret that our presence
today / was unwelcome, I want to say again that our intention
was to –

M. And what are you, are you, what, insurance? Armour? The
progressive face? Can't say we're all big country thicks picking
up girls on the game for freebies, we HAVE a girl and she's
Black and all?

G. I don't appreciate being talked about that way.

M. Oh you don't do you not? You don't like being talked about?
Did he take the photos as well? / Was that you?

P. No, that wasn't – /

G. DON'T – /

M. Maybe it wasn't you but you know, don't you? You know
who did, and you know we're going to find out sooner or later
because we're not going to stop, we're not going to sleep, and
you won't fucking say and save us that after all you've already
gone and done.

–

You won't even say sorry, will you.

G. –

Everyone deeply regrets what has happened.

G *begins a dance that slowly grows more and more strenuous
and exuberant both.*

M. {In the umbra of death it's hard to remember the things you
want to}

P. It is unclear if the Garda concerned has returned to work or

M. {The picture we want out there the picture we're using

It's from the year she was doing really well

Ran the minimarathon for the DRCC

Healthy her meds working her hair done just a little while back

Didn't mind her teeth as much and colour from the sun}

P. And with regards to prosecution or disciplinary action

M. {It's easy to remember the three-in-the-morning calls

From her and you half-wished you could've hung up

Or from hospital and dressing wishing she'd've called

Harder to remember heavy rain on Clonea Beach

Ages eighteen and twenty-eight and she says giz the car keys

I'll run back drive here save you the walk or don't you trust me}

P. Regretfully cannot comment on ongoing internal inquiries

M. {We walked an hour she's gone twenty back driving giddy with
it

Laughing at the run she ran skinsoaked in the driver's seat

Steaming but still wetter than you and you've been standing in it

From when we were kids she could run and run and run

Stayed skinny and flat her whole life so sometimes

You're talking she's out the door in jeans gone an hour

Loved it kept her sane she said loads of times

She's registered for the minimarathon this year again

Haven't had the heart yet to phone them say that

Preventative is one word another is

What I want to know is

What I want you to tell me if you can is

What did you prevent?

Because they never get a chance to do it, did they?

So we never get to know, do we?

G *hits a peak in the dance.*

The picture we want out there the picture we're using

It's from the year she was doing really well

Would she have run it in forty like she wanted to maybe

In my head there's a universe

It keeps going around in my head that somewhere

You didn't do what you did and she's alive

And I don't get to live there because you did do what you did}

The End.

WHERE SAT THE LOVERS

Carys D. Coburn
with MALAPROP THEATRE

Introduction

This is a show about a group of people who all, for one reason or another, have an urgent need to come up with a story that explains the big scary world around them. For some of them that's about the political situation they were born into without consultation. For some it's about their family, ditto on the no consultation beforehand. Some of them are told they have a disease because of this need they share with all the others. Some of them are dead, depending on your interpretation of what you're about to see – or have just seen. We started off making a show about codes, pivoted to making a show about information, had to forbid ourselves from writing Caryl Churchill's *Love and Information* because she's already written it, and ended up zooming in on a human irony at the heart of all the abstractions that had attracted us in the first place: most of us want to be seen and be safe all at once, but the more we touch the world, the more it touches us back. Seeking one loses you the other. The warmth of someone's attention comes from friction, which comes with the potential for injury. That's rich, we thought. Let's explore that.

Where the show steps beyond this irony and the characters who live it, it's not because our interest has lapsed. It's because we want to show you the world they are trying to make sense of. Or failing that, because trying to put a whole world on stage is necessarily doomed to fail sooner or later, stages like maps being smaller than the territories the model, we want to capture something of what their world feels like. The moments of spectacle, of abstraction, of conceptual weirdness, are snapshots of the landscape of the characters' inquiry.

The problem of putting a whole world on stage is one we share with all kinds of non-narrative/post-dramatic/idea-driven theatre. With character-driven theatre, you stop the show when interesting things stop happening to the character. When you're mapping all the places a rich idea touches other rich ideas, it can be hard to know when to stop. Notes-app apologies get you to sincerity which gets you to Protestantism which gets you to the reformation which gets you to the printing press which gets you to oral peasant culture, and so on, and so on, and so on, and when will you have finally said enough? When will the audience finally understand enough?

Looked at it this way, we can see why one of the definitive gestures of this type of theatre is the cacophony, the burst of chaos, the moment when every major image from the show thus far is superimposed and magnified while loud music plays and things drop from the ceiling and probably someone gets covered in fake blood or feathers or both. It's a cyst of the sublime, a bounded instant of incomprehensible scale – there's too much going on for us to track, so we can't piece it all together because we never get a hold of it in the first place. Cacophony affords an ending which is abrupt but not arbitrary – it reminds us that if and when we are offered a fuller truth we can't grasp it fully, so there would be no point in continuing indefinitely to try to understand. And if we have to stop at some point, why not now? Cacophony reconciles us to the partiality of our knowledge, lacking anything better.

When these moments work, you could call them a kind of failed transcendence – a gesture towards complete comprehension which pointedly, necessarily, falls short. When they don't work, when they feel cursory, arbitrary, like the makers ran out of time and threw a load of gas shit together and hoped you wouldn't mind because you like 'Cut to the Feeling' by Carly Rae Jepsen and it's playing at 140 decibels, you could call these moments of failed failed transcendence – the piece tries to refuse its authority even as it forbids us from asking any of the questions we're left with. ENOUGH, I don't understand and neither do you – stop trying to. The principled refusal of closure becomes a closure itself when we shift from asking questions we can't answer definitively, once and for all, to not asking questions, full stop. (As though contingent answers are as bad as no answers at all.)

The ending of this show is a cousin of cacophony. We could have gone with a straightforward cacophony; arguably, it will never be more thematic and justified than in a piece about conspiracy theory, secret history, pathologies of meaning both public and private, sociological and neuronal. But instead of failing to fail to have authority, we're trying to offer false false comfort; we want to whisper a thought to you that you know you should disbelieve, but can't quite because you don't want to. We hope that's nice for you, even if it's something else as well.

Where Sat the Lovers was first performed at Project Arts Centre, Dublin, on 22 September 2021, as part of Dublin Fringe Festival. The cast was as follows:

E	Juliette Crosbie
F	Bláithín MacGabhann
G	Maeve O'Mahony
ISAAC NEWTON	Wren Dennehy

Writer	Carys D. Coburn
	with MALAPROP
Director	Claire O'Reilly
Set and Costume Design	Molly O'Cathain
Lighting Design	John Gunning
Sound Design	Jennifer O'Malley
	Leon Henry
Stage Manager	Rachael Kivlehan
Assistant Stage Manager	Olivia Drennan
Producer	Carla Rogers
Production Manager	Grace Halton

Supported by the Arts Council, Dublin City Council, Cork Midsummer Festival, Carlow Arts Festival, Project Arts Centre and field:arts.

Characters

E
F
G
ISAAC NEWTON

Note on the Dialogue

A dash (–) at the end of a line indicates an interruption from the next speaker.

A slash (/) indicates overlapping dialogue.

Isaac One

ISAAC NEWTON, *immortal time-travelling drag king, appears and begins to preach. Seeing as he was the flamboyant and fringe Protestant of his day, he can be the contemporary equivalent – a kind of super-pastor, moving freely between speech and song as the Word moves him.*

The following text is a kind of speaking in tongues, aboth in the sense of an ecstatic babbling AND in the sense that it's supposed to touch the heart of the listener directly without passing through the mind. First. It's hallucinatory, conspiratorial in that discomfiting way when someone addresses you knowingly on the presumption that you are also privy to some secret meaning – but you're not.

I. I could say France.

I could say King James the Ant.

I could say Eamonn DeValera was a good mother to you and to you and to you. Did he give you the breast? Did he give you the bottle? Did he make you a coddle?

Oh I could say Jesus was a woman, not a man but a woman, would that affect your religious beliefs if I told you that Jesus was a woman?

I could say when I say I could say when I say I could say

Repeat, ad-lib and segue into speaking the following call and responses with the audience. The freer ISAAC feels to get outrageous and campy with them, ad-libbing flirty asides and encouragements and endearments, the better.

When I say Isaac You say Newton

Isaac

When I say equal you say opposite

Equal

When I say laws of you say gravity

Laws of

When I say inverse you square law

Inverse

I *subsides and basks in the attention they are getting.*

I'm not going to lie, I love that I'm the only person everyone can see

And I don't mind that I can't see everyone back, because I trust you to only think nice things

F *enters the space.*

And now everyone can see them, but no one can see all of them

Some of you can see their face, some of you can see their back

Some of you can see they're bricking it

No one can see that their underwear is green

That they haven't worn an underwire bra in two years

That they haven't had sex in three

That they don't wank as much as they used to, since trying those meds broke their routine

There is no position where all of things are visible because some of them aren't, is the point

So seeing and thinking are partly guessing, is the point

No one can see they're ashamed of it now, but they (F.) they wanted to go to Oxford or Cambridge before they knew what they wanted to study.

Like, fucking Kill Me Now embarrassing.

And then they were caught between, they wanted to be a composer but they also wanted to not die homeless.

So they saved and saved, waited to be a mature student, went Up to Cambridge for Uni to Read Architecture and write music on the side.

They wrote this. (*Music plays.*)

What you're hearing now is the title of this show in Morse code. (*This should be true.*)

The high notes are longs and shorts, the low notes are dividers, the pitches change when it's a new word.

People mostly don't notice, which is why I'm telling you.

To make sure you appreciate how cool this is.

That even if you can't feel the meaning the way you can feel the meaning in what I'm saying, it's there.

They like codes, they used to write a lot of pieces like this.

At some point in the preceding, E *has entered.*

And then they went to see *Arrival* in the cinema, which ruined their entire fucking life.

Hookup

E. So I'm not going to ask is this a hookup, because when we were messaging it was very clear, like I know I didn't misunderstand, and your music is Great but, but I'll ask you if, does a hookup not mean having sex to you?

F. No it does

E. Because it's cool if you just want to chat and like, Get To Know Each Other, but I thought that we were, / you know

F. No I want to

E. Yeah?

F. Or thought we were going to, but now that you're here –

E. Oh

F. And you're hot! Hotter in person even, I'm not saying –

E. Saw you in real life, portcullis down –

F. God no

E. Well, fucking phew

F. I'm nervous, is what I mean, it's been a while for me.

E. Yeah, me too

F. Hard to believe

E. Shut up

   Pause.

F. Do you want anything? / Sorry I didn't offer

E. Like, wine?

F. There's no wine

E. Okay

F. Any booze, actually

E. Okay

F. I shouldn't drink

E. No judgement!

   –

   Who's this? (*Picture of Isaac Newton.*)

F. Isaac Newton

E. And who's this? (*Fatio.*)

F. Newton's boyf

E. No way! He was – [gay? Into boys?]

F. Big time

E. Who knew?

F. Me

E. And what's this? (*Waveform.*)

F. The complete waveform of 'Barbie Girl' by Aqua

E. Banger, and I guess that's 'Doctor Jones'? (*Another waveform.*)

F. It actually is

E. No fucking way!

F. Fucking way

E. Proud of myself, and what's this? (*A working miniature optical telegraph.*)

F. It's a working miniature optical telegraph

E. Beep boop beep boop

F. That's a telegram, an electrical telegram

E. Fucking duh, that's the electric noise

F. I didn't want to say it

E. I'm such a jock

F. But this is analogue, just moving parts, and the position of the arms tells you what it says

E. What does it say?

F. Whatever you want it to, seven times seven positions / for the small arms times four positions for the big arm gives –

E. I meant right now, what's that shape say

F. One hundred and ninety-six, oh, that's an L

E. For Loch Ness Monster (*Because it looks like one, see Chappe code.*)

F. Or locrian

E (*mishearing*). Loch Rian?

F. Locrian, it's a musical scale?

E (*being a dumb bitch on purpose*). Or, lezzers

F (*trying for playful*). Or, licking?

E. Hot

F. Or, Large, or, Long – [Tongue? Fingers? Eyelashes? Who the fuck knows]?

E. –

And what's this? (*A picture.*)

F. It's a long exposure of trains switching at Great Victoria Street

E. You'd want to be careful

F. Yeah?

E. Taking photos of train stations, particularly if, you were there with your camera for a while for this?

F. Three-hour exposure yeah, is that bad?

E. Is it bad to hang around Belfast visibly surveilling the public transport system?

F. Okay

E. I'm kind of scared to ask now, but this is – ?

F. Larne Road Carrickfergus

E. –

　　And?

F. And?

E. And why is it Larne Road Carrickfergus?

F. It's where the police archive was until it 'mysteriously' burned
　　down in 1990

E. She's brought out the quotemarks!

F. I promise I'm not a lizardpeople person

E. No?

F. Because come on, it's just facts that we don't know everything
　　that the RUC were up to back then, the people they were
　　working with admitted they were working with them even if
　　they still deny it, Loughinisland inquiry confirmed it and back
　　in the day when a big investigation was starting all the records
　　burn down and none of the fire alarms are working, it'd be
　　weirder if that were a coincidence, or am I fucking crazy?

E. –

　　It's the PSNI now

F. Right, but 1990 they're the RUC, aren't they?

E. You tell me, expert who isn't a lizard

F. Or a lizardpeople person

E. Or that, and what's this? (*A photo.*)

F. It's a picture of fingernail scratches on the walls of a gas chamber

E. –

F. But not in a, I know the Holocaust happened

E. Glad to hear it

F. This all looks bad

E. No

F. But it's an art project, cross my heart

E. Though didn't the Nazis blow them up?

F. Which?

E. The ones they bring you to, school trips for posh schools with blazers I mean, but if you go on a tour of the camps now then the gas chambers are reconstructions because they blew them up when they were losing the war, right?

F. You're not – [a Holocaust denier]?

E. My dad's Jewish

F. Cool

E. And also I'm not a Holocaust denier

F. Good

E. You sure?

F. If only because I wouldn't have sex with you

E. Policy is important

F. Though I think you're right, they're reconstructions, but this photo's from the room in the crematorium where they trialled murdering people with gas before scaling that up

E. Which is –

F. Still there?

E. Yeah

F. Yeah

E. It leaves the question though, I was sort of with you up to train stations and police headquarters, but now I'm a bit –

F. What's it all for?

E. Yeah

F. I'm still working it out myself

E. So you're not going to tell me?

F. I can't, I know there's a connection between all this but I haven't worked out what it is yet, sounds wanky but true

E. –

By the way, my ex was in recovery so I'm really used to dates without, none of that spooks me basically

F. Alcohol?

E. Because weren't you saying?

F. That I don't drink?

E. Or am I a presumptuous cunt?

F. No, I did, but I'm not in recovery

E. –

You're not Presbyterian?

F. –

Sexiest hookup ever, right? But I should probably, up front, it's cleaner if I just tell you, my sister thinks I'm a voice hearer

E. A voice hearer?

F. Like, what used to be called schizophrenic

E. Okay

F. Though, being exact, the clever money was on schizoaffective for me

E. Very different?

F. The tasteful joke is, the police kill schizophrenics and schizoaffectives kill themselves

E. –

You said that's what your sister thinks?

F. Yeah

E. Wouldn't you know better than her?

F. I say, I had one episode half a decade ago and I've been fine since

E. Episode like – [what]?

F. Episode like, went to see a film about talking to aliens, couldn't get out of bed the next morning, day after that couldn't understand when people were speaking to me, month in an English hospital, didn't finish my degree

E. –

I'm sorry

F. Me too, but like I said, stay away from alcohol for the mood stuff and sci-fi films for the dissociative psychosis stuff and I'm fine

E. Okay

F. And never formally diagnosed!

E. No?

F. Very over hospitals

E. Fair

F. Yeah?

E. But did you – ?

F. Yeah?

E. It's called, you may or may not be A Voice Hearer –

F. Did I hear voices?

E. Good way of knowing one way or another, no?

F. –

I heard all sorts

E. Okay

F –

Do you want to leave?

E. No!

F. Because, least fucking sexy thing to fucking say, but I have legal capacity, I can consent, I'm living with my sister because money not because I need CONSTANT SURVEILLANCE / to make sure I don't drink bleach

E. Did you tell me you live with your sister?

F. –

Did I not?

E. She's not going to walk in, is she?

F. She works nights in a hotel, which was part of it, I got priced out of Dublin and she's barely here, / not really meant for two but if one of the two is on reverse time –

E. Because, don't know about you, that's not really my – [Kink? Vibe? Thing?]

F. Just not sexy, no

E. –

Is there another bedroom somewhere I'm not seeing?

F. No

E. So we'd be fucking on the couch?

F. I actually sleep in the bedroom, she sleeps on the couch because, / with work and all

E. She's barely here

F. Yeah

E. Okay

F. –

This is fucked, I've fucked it so bad, you can go, I understand

E. –

What's this? (*A photo.*)

F. –

That is, you should know actually, you've seen them already, but that is my tits

E. Secretly built by aliens, were they?

F. Shut up

E. They're fucking hot

F. –

Yeah?

E. You're fucking hot

Isaac Two

ISAAC *call and responses, again he is free to riff:*

I. I say Newton You say Genius

I say Genius You say Alchemist

I say Alka You say Hest

I say Philosopher's You say Stone

I say Arian You say Heresy

I say There's No You say Trinity

I say Jesus You say Man

I say The Father You say Divine

I say Consensus You say Reality

I say Diana You Say Murdered

I say Blue Ivy You Say Solange's

I say Schizo You say Phrenia

I say Folk Belief and Memory

You say Site of Inchoate Anticapitalist Resistance

Check Against Video

Hi, I'm Isaac Newton, and has this ever happened to you?

You look at an egg and you think Wow, eggs are closed.

Nothing in, nothing out, so if you think about it, it's already a chicken.

(*TED-talk voice implying this is a profound insight.*) It's just In. The. Wrong. Order.

When we break an egg and whisk it we call it scrambling, but actually when we scramble an egg we're keeping it in a functionally identical Non. Chicken. State.

So really, isn't it chickens that are really scrambled?

Isn't a chicken the configuration of an egg that makes it really new, even though nothing new has been added?

Maybe you're thinking, what's with this guy!

Did he accidentally take a whole week's worth of psilocybin microdoses?

But I am neither straight nor tripping.

Just ask Leibniz about those dick pics I sent him!

I don't fancy him, I am gay, I'm not ashamed, but it was a humiliation thing.

What I'm saying is, I'm not not making sense, you just don't know enough to make sense of the sense I'm making.

Which might be a familiar feeling for you, if you love someone who tells you   things that sound like conspiracy theories.

Which might, in fact, BE conspiracy theories.

Or might be accurate descriptions of the actual conspiracies that governments are allowed have.

But because the conspiracies are, you know, conspiratorial, we never know enough to know the difference between the founded and the false for sure.

It's definitional, darlings.

That we're usually more or less right to allege conspiracy, and we're usually more or less wrong about the specifics.

But it's hard to know the exact ratio of right to wrong, sensical to nonsensical.

I could say, for example, that under US governance nearly forty per cent of Puerto Rican women were sterilised by 1970

I could say the RUC colluded with the UVF in the Loughinisland Massacre

I could say SWAT teams were created to destroy the Black Panthers

I could say the gas chambers are reconstructions

I could say that Hillary Clinton is a paedophile

I could say all priests are paedophiles

I could say that Arthur C. Clarke was a paedophile

I could say Jesus was a man, not divine, so there's no Trinity

I could say France has assassinated twenty-two African presidents since 1963

I could say Jesus was a woman

Siblings

F *is listening to one of their Morse code pieces of music, G is waiting to start a conversation*

G. Which one is this?

> (*Listens.*)

> Was that an L?

> (*Listens.*)

> O

> (*Listens.*)

> V, is this the Edgar Allen Poe one?

F. I don't believe you

G. Sorry?

F. Like maybe it was silly of me to put codes in my music so people would have to listen more carefully, when actually the simple harmony meant people just tuned it out like some shit with panpipes they'd have on in a spa, didn't listen at all, but even if they DID listen more carefully what's the REAL weak link?

G. –

F. Instruments! You have to write all the pieces for the same instrument or they just remember which bit of coded text is which ensemble. String quartet is the Emily Dickinson poem, horn and electronics is Mary Oliver, solo piano is the Edgar Allen Poe cipher, like the Nazis having an unbreakable code but starting every message with Heil Hitler, which is why, don't try and start a conversation by pretending you're suddenly really into my music because, A, I know you already know, and B, since when can you actually keep up?

G. –

> So bluntly, because it has to be, if I'm tactful you'll just pretend you're stupider than you are and don't understand, which by the way, total double standard that no one is allowed to condescend to you because You Went To Cambridge, like I don't fucking know, but then whenever you don't want to have a conversation it's Sorry Me No Language You Talk Me You Bully Me, but

to just, saying it straight out I think you're slipping, and I'm scared, and I think / you should see someone

F. Healthcare is violence

G. Yeah but, okay, once we're at healthcare is violence so is, tell me how not eating or sleeping for two days isn't a violent thing to do to yourself

F. Sometimes I can't sleep

G. And sometimes you Don't eat, and now is sometimes, and if we both think really fucking hard we might think of a reason you Just Happen to be turning into a stick insect, I go to work, you're sitting at your laptop playing music you wrote five years ago, I come home, you're sitting at your laptop playing music you wrote five years ago, I make sure the fridge is full for you and I end up throwing away bags of slime, I make you things and you don't eat them so I end up eating vegan lasagne three days running even though I'm not fucking vegan, no reason for any of that no? / None of that paints a picture for you

F. Reasons, okay, reasons, I'm poor, we live in an occupied territory that just came through a pandemic where policy was Let Them Die / the planet's literally on fire

G. I'm sure the Fenian dead are VERY appreciative of your acoustic cover of the hunger strikes, / Bobby Sands thumbsupping in heaven

F. Even if I'm mentally ill, / all I'm saying is that if you're not freaked you're not paying attention

G. If? If I still had my old phone I'd play you some of the voicenotes you left me, then two weeks thinking you're dead because nothing, / can't drop everything and fly over because I don't know where you are

F. It wasn't personal or, it wasn't on purpose, deliberate, I was basically non-verbal

G. And this is what's, this here, I'm fine but I was non-verbal, hospitals are evil but the government's eviler for not building more of them during Covid, / explain that to me

F. I've never said it didn't happen, that I didn't, and I've said I'm sorry you were scared, true or false

G. True

F. And I went to the place in Dublin, true or false

G. True

F. And they said I had PTSD and wanted to know who raped me because someone must have, true or false

G. True, they were horrible and didn't listen, but you didn't go back to herself who you SAID you liked either, true or false

F. False, I couldn't, because they copped / it wasn't my student card

G. You weren't a student, oh yeah

F. So there

G. But the very first time, back home, you just never renewed your prescription when it was working and all, true or false

F. False

G. False yourself

F. False, they tripled my dosage

G. –

    I didn't know that

F. No you didn't, because you don't listen, and neither did yer man when I said my dosage was perfect, but I tried the new ones and I was nauseous for six months coming on them, remember that? Me getting sick all the time?

G. Yeah

F. Dropped two stone, had to stop taking them to gain some weight back, six months' nausea coming off them as well, hadn't eaten anything but potato fucking waffles in a year because everything else had me gawking my ring up, looked at the prescription and said fuck that, that's what you want me to go back to, is it?

G. Obviously not

F. It'd simplify the shopping list, waffles waffles waffles waffles waffles waffles waffles waffles / waffles waffles waffles waffles waffles waffles waffles

G. OKAY

F. And true or false, you never mention the guy who said I COULDN'T have schizoaffective because I have no delusions of reference, / true or false

G. Obsessed with codes, writes Morse code music, no delusions of reference, okay

F. This is why I hate how you talk about all this, I don't have a personality, I'm just symptoms, everything's evidence, my art is evidence, my politics are evidence, I was writing music with codes for years before all the, before Cambridge, and to you that's Proof that it was Going To Happen, so what isn't Proof, is it Proof that I didn't eat green things or never slept even when we were kids, you put on your Aqua tape to put you to sleep and then I'm stuck listening to the whole thing, / or maybe that's the cause of it all, overexposure to fucking 'Barbie Girl'

G. I know, I know, I know, I know, I know, I know, I know, you didn't start calling people bootlickers because you're sick, / you started calling people,

F. Had an episode /

G. HAD AN EPISODE, excuse me, you got all Fuck The Brits Twenty-Six Plus Six Kill The Landlords Health Under Capitalism Is Just Being Exploitable because sourest grapes ever, if you don't get to graduate from Cambridge then anyone else who does is a fucking nazi Obviously, you don't hate the empire you hate not being the emperor

F. Why Cambridge?

G. You fucking tell me, I wasn't obsessed with going

F. No, why was I fine until I went to Cambridge?

G. Typical onset is between sixteen and thirty

F. Is that an answer?

G. What are you, just tell me what this is

F. Sixteen to thirty, okay, why not sixteen? Why not seventeen? / Why not eighteen? Why not nineteen? Why not twenty? Why not twenty-one? Why not twenty-two? Why not twenty-three? Why twenty-four?

G. Alcohol, weed, stress, you say it yourself, I don't fucking know

F. Because Cambridge, posh cunts toasting the Queen and it's not a joke, everyone Irish is wearing tweed, I had a toxic response to a toxic environment, / no Chemical Imbalance or Genetic Predisposition needed to explain it

G. And now? Why are you not, what's wrong now? What is it this time?

F. I'm thirty and I share a one-bedroom with my sister in Belfast, the Buckfast Gulag, come for the absolutely fuck-all / and stay for the generational trauma

G. No one made you move here

F. No one would let me suck their dick for a studio in Dublin either

G. Exactly, okay it's Toxic but it's Less toxic, cheaper, rent and healthcare, meds, not that that fucking matters if you won't even put yourself on the waiting list

F. –

Is that why you invited me up?

G. –

I was worried about you, yes

F. But to try and get me treated again?

G. That's violence as well, is it?

F. I thought you just meant rent

G. That too

F. You sneaky bitch

G. –

So Cambridge, toxic, Dublin, toxic, Belfast, toxic, where would you be well?

F. It's my fault that everywhere's shit?

G. If it's places, if your genes or your brain aren't anything, if it's places and every place is toxic why isn't everyone fucked in the head?

F. If it's me, my stuff my genes, why aren't you fucked in the head?

G. If it's places, why isn't everyone in Cambridge fucked in the head?

F. Everyone in Cambridge IS fucked in the head

G. Why aren't they fucked in the head like you're fucked in the head then

F. Different sicknesses because different lives, different bruises, different sensitivities, / levels of sensitivity even

G. Okay so life history, we grew up together, same bedroom, same Aqua tape, why amn't I fucked in the head?

F. Please, don't ask me that, / it's too tempting

G. Or, okay, if you won't engage, we grow up together, we both have both our parents kill themselves within five years of each other, you have problems, that doesn't suggest a genetic component to you?

F. –

She didn't kill herself

G. Sorry, you're right, she liked REM so much that she couldn't resist going night-swimming / IN HER CLOTHES after sinking a bottle of Baileys, no pun intended

F. But to answer, I say it's about traumas, you talk about them dying, you don't see how that's, that that's more than a bruise, a gash, a wound, whatever but just major? I took the call about him.

G. And I took hers

F. But I had to do all that stuff with the police because he used a gun

G. I did too, I just didn't refuse to answer them like a fucking tool

F. There you go

G. What?

F. Different experiences, you're obedient police like you, different bruises, police don't like me, different problems, no genes

G. You really think how you are, that it's all HOW they died?

F. Why does there have to be one big reason?

G. You're asking me?

F. Why is, what's so hard for you about The World Is Hard So I Find It Hard?

G. Well my question is, they're dead and you're sick and that's the One Coincidence you believe is a coincidence? Everything else is capitalism or colonialism or the New World Order but you Just Happen to be a sick person with two parents who committed, who died violently?

–

I wish you'd go to hospital

F. I'd rather drink bleach

G. And much as I'd love the chance to declutter, have a living room again, that's what I'm really really scared of

–

I'm terrified for you, and of you, to the point, sometimes when my shift's over I sit with everyone while they drink, two three hours extra pretending to listen to Jake's not very hot takes about Quentin Tarantino, six a.m. and the sun's coming up and I can get the bus back, that long, because when I'm coming up the stairs I have this knot in my stomach, that I'm going to open the door, I'm thinking what if it's this time?

F. I've never hurt myself

G. That you believe, that you say that is what's terrifying, and to me, sometimes, like with Cambridge, it's, do you actually think the NHS is the boot of the empire or do you just think you're too good for it? Like, on some level, is it That's How You Treat Nutjobs and Morons Fine But I Am NOT A Nutjob Moron?

F. You're yelling

G. I'm not fucking yelling

F. And it's, I can't, I'm stressed

G. –

I'm sorry

A moment while F tries to settle and G lets them, then decides to help.

On the bus the other day, realised I was singing that little melody from your piece

Sings a snippet, which should have the rhythmic shape short long short long short, i.e. A–R in Morse.

Is that right?

F *shakes their head.*

Can you sing it? What should it be?

F *hums what it should be.*

Okay, and I remember you said E is the most common letter in English, is that an E?

F *shakes their head.*

Or is a word like An or The or, just really common?

F *shakes their head.*

Or is it the W from the title, is that why I hear it so much?

F. A and an R

G. Are there loads of those?

F. In Early, and Warm, and Share, and Are, and Various, and Ardent, six of them, so more common than any other bigram except the ones in The, and E is just Dot so you don't hear it

G. What's a bigram?

F. Two letters in a row

G. Cool

F. Did I tell you, before the optical telegraph the brothers the Chappe brothers, their system, they tried two synchronised clocks with letters around the edge

F *mimes the hand going around on a clock and enlists G to mime the other clock moving in lockstep with theirs.*

and you, the idea was you fire a gun when the hand is on the letter you want, they hear it, write down your letter, A B C D

F *makes a gunshot noise.*

E!

F *looks at G expectantly until they 'write down' an E.*

G. Yeah?

F. See a problem?

G. Bullets?

F. Right, slow, expensive, hard to explain to the neighbours, so then they were just shouting to each other instead (*Shouts*.) E!

G. But if you can hear each other anyway – [what's the point?]

F. Right? It's really good communication for people who don't need to communicate, saying things you don't need to say, which is, that's, I like that

G. Can't think why

F. –

> *Precise and difficult shift in performance needs to happen here; whenever anyone talks naturally they take the stairs a few at a time, because they know they don't have to spell out everything on the basis that anyone who speaks the language they're speaking is also familiar with the world they're speaking about. (Imagine having to explain what an apple was every time you said the word 'apple'.) So what happens to F's speech over the next page or so isn't what you'd call a 'breakdown' so much as it is a building up, an increase in what they're prepared to leave latent on the confident assumption that it's pretty clear what they mean. They're no different from anyone else in the assumption itself, they're just a bit more optimistic than most people. At first, until they see how G is responding to them, they would be surprised if someone didn't understand them.*

And there was a woman on the ward, my thing was, or I kept thinking, I kept thinking oh her skin, and the cuts, the cuts are a shame, her age, so good, and then wait, did I expect, what did I expect just because, but she says I shouldn't be here, she says over and over, they know me in Springbank, I have BPD I'm not, I was drunk when I, they know me, and the prick, I've told you, the prick, / he's a prick

G. Sweetheart, you're – [slipping.]

F. He says No beds in Springbank sweetheart, just the way, when you call me because, and she hates it too, this day, second day, this day, or third, this day she hits him, YOU FUCKING CREEP, in a room on her own, no restraints allowed, the Act, any more no, so no locks, he's sitting on the floor in front, she's banging, holding it, holding it shut, hours, won't let her out, falls asleep

G. He did?

F. In the room, they carry her out

G. Fuck

F. Next, he's on shift, maybe tomorrow, does it again

G. Which?

F. Calls her, she loses it, doesn't like sweetheart, way he touches your shoulder, or says it

G. Why?

F. She sleeps through

G. Through the night?

F. Doesn't wake up, calmer, easier for him

G. For them? For the staff?

F. –

   Slipping

Isaac Three

I. No one can see them (F.) in the toilet, which is why they sometimes sit until they start worrying about haemorrhoids

   There's nothing to do except wait to need to go again, but that feels weirdly like freedom

   They have all the power they want as long as they don't try to do anything with it

   Other things no one sees about their sister:

   That she pinches herself to make herself take phonecalls

   That she uses the company of friends as an excuse to just not answer, and she's happy to let them think it's because she values her time with them

   That she thinks she's come to terms with her parents' sudden violent deaths in quick succession, provided nothing reminds her of the first two thirds of her life

Other things no one sees about their hookup from the other week:

That she compulsively looks at photos of her ex with their new person, whose haircut she would love to have but is worried work wouldn't allow

That she made a profile that is not identifiably her to be able to look at those photos

That she thinks about ringing her ex to say You Never TOLD Me You Wanted To Get A Dog, WE Could Have Had A Dog

If you think about it, pretty much everything that happens goes unobserved, unconsidered, ununderstood, by anyone

Except me, but I'm a narrative convenience

Or a ghost

Or the sanctified flesh of the hallowed soul of Sir Isaac Newton, immortal ever since I cracked the recipe for the Philosopher's Stone

I'll give you a hint: it's not bees.

But before we go any further, the elephant in the room.

The allegations.

Not that kind!

I'm not Kevin Spacey!

But some people think I'm a crackpot, just because I, like Archbishop Cranmer and Ian Paisley, believe the Pope is the Antichrist.

ISAAC *reveals that under his baroque outer clothes he is wearing a T shirt that says 'POPE JOHN PAUL II ANTICHRIST'.*

Merch on sale in the foyer after the show.

But I'm not a crackpot for predicting the world will end in twenty-sixty, because One, look the fuck around, and Two, the pope is CLEARLY the Antichrist.

And Revelations CLEARLY states that the Antichrist will reign for twelve-hundred-sixty days.

And twelve-hundred-sixty DAYS is CLEARLY a code for twelve-hundred-sixty YEARS.

And twenty-sixty is CLEARLY twelve-hundred-sixty years after the year eight hundred – MATHS – when Holy Roman Emperor Charlemagne bestowed legitimacy on Pepin's donation of lands to the Papacy, which corrupted the spiritual purity of the Papacy by making the Pope a temporal king.

Spits.

Hence, you know.

ISAAC *indicates their T-shirt.*

You could say why count from Charlemagne's thumbs up for Pepin and not just Pepin, Isaac?

You could say why not count from seven fifty-six and say the apocalypse should have been in twenty sixteen but wasn't, the world is still doing fine?

And I could say, is it?

Is it really?

You could say, stick to the science, Isaac baby.

And I could say but here's the thing, science didn't exist when I was young and not so dumb but VERY full of cum.

So I wasn't doing science when I was formalising gravity and rimming trade in molly houses, I was doing natural philosophy.

And natural philosophy's whole thing was deciphering God's intention from the book of his creation.

So no biblical exegesis no inertia, baby.

No alchemy no mass times acceleration.

No Antichrist no for every action an equal and opposite reaction, no inverse square law, no planetary orbits, no Moon landing, though needless to say there was no Moon landing.

No staring at the sun until my eyes burned no nothing because we're not closed like eggs.

We can't be ourselves until we let something else come inside us.

If you haven't tried it, you're missing out.

Except you have tried it, whatever you think.

You might like to think the self is a sealed box, a castle, a safe safe.

But I could say your ears are holes.

I could say your skin is litmus.

I could say the eye burns on purpose, and the burns spell out prophecies of what the skin will soon feel.

I could say we're all being barebacked by radio wave transmissions right now.

I could say information is the difference that makes a difference

I could say knowledge is anything that leaves a mark

I could say meaning is a scar

Quartet

F *now has an intrusive bulky apparatus – a home-made Lissajous pendulum. It takes up a lot of living-room space. F has just finished making a disgusting microwave-egg concoction for* G.

F. Here

G. Thank you

–

Is it – [supposed to be like this] ?

F. Scrambled eggs

G. Right

The door buzzer goes, G *goes to answer it. F faffs with their apparatus. In our production, they put on 'Barbie Girl' to try and be cute and it played diegetically until* E*'s entrance below.* G *comes back.*

Do you know why the police would be visiting?

F. No?

> F *starts ineffectually trying to clear the apparatus away.*

G. Can I help?

F. No

G. If it'd be faster

F. No

G. I'll just move your clothes then, will I?

F. Those are yours

G. I'll move them

F. Do

G. Okay they're coming up, I'm asking nicely, / please just take down the fucking whatever it is

F. So it's too late, it takes ages to take apart and then I'll be here for ages putting it back, / which if you want space is worse than just leaving it alone

G. You're not setting it back up after, Jesus Christ

> E *enters in uniform as a PSNI officer.*

F. You're a police officer?

E. Will I close the door?

G. Is your partner – [coming in]?

F. You're a police officer

E (*to* F.) Yes – (*To* G.) he's having a smoke, don't want anyone to feel too, this is a very low-key visit so no need to feel scrutinised, or – [threatened]?

G. You can leave it open in case, / air if nothing else

F. Fuck's sake

E. Will we sit down?

G (*to* F.) What is wrong with you? (*To* E.) My sibling, who is Very polite today, has also filled the room with creepy bullshit / so there actually isn't room to pull out the chairs

F. Which is good, it's Good because she's not staying

E (*to* F). What's the optical telegram say today?

G. Are optical telegrams having a Moment?

F. It's a telegraph, / an optical telegraph

E. But the reason I'm, this isn't an interview but I wanted to informally, very gently, ask you if you know anything about someone with a Cork accent who followed two officers from near here, Artana I think they said, across the river and most of the way down the Ormeau Road recording them on their phone, bold move, / particularly if you believe them that they were shouting stuff the whole time

G (*to* F). Tell me this isn't real /

F. And what? /

E. Racist Fucking Pricks was the standout, which sounded like you I thought

G. You know each other?

F. They stopped that girl for no fucking reason, or not no reason the reason is, they see a Black girl running down the road and thinks she looks a bit too happy, a bit too Not Worried, and they don't like that, or are you going to try tell me she didn't look twelve and they seriously thought she was asking people on the street if they wanted their dicks sucked?

E. And if that's true, I'm sure she's Really glad that you've made them angry

G. How do you know each other?

F. Jesus fucking Christ would you, we hooked up a few weeks back and I never heard from her, / guess we know why now

E. I didn't hear from you either

G. Sorry, YOU hooked up with a POLICE OFFICER?

F. She hid that

E. Sorry, who hid what?

G. You fucking hypocrite

F. She didn't tell me

E. I would have the next time, but then I thought you were embarrassed about how things went / and didn't want a next time so I'd leave it

G. Don't need to know, really don't need to know

F (*to* G). Would you grow up?

E (*to* F). Fuck, are you not out?

G (*to* E). I'm not a homophobe, I just don't need to know what they do in my bed

F (*to* E). Of course I'm out, and I wasn't embarrassed, (*To* G.) and I don't do anything on YOUR bed that you don't do in OUR shower and I didn't have a total fanny attack when you left a fucking DILDO / in there the other week, so, fuck, what is going on?

G. A toy, NOT a dildo, a TOY

E. –

 (*To* G.) You can go if you're uncomfortable, but I didn't mean, nothing X-rated, (*To* F.) I just meant that you talked about yourself for like two hours before and after you kicked me out really early, so, I don't know, but talking more is one reason I'm here

G. Gas

F (*to* G). I think you Should fuck off actually

E. Might be easier all round, this is a bit – [weird uncomfortable? complicated?]

G. –

 I don't think they should be left alone with you

F. I'm not a fucking child

E. They aren't

G. Well it's my house

 They look at her.

 I'm going to steal one smoke off her partner and smoke it, and by then you'll have said sorry, won't ever happen again, and it won't, and your stupid fucking sand thing [laser thing] (*She should say whatever is appropriate for the Lissajous-apparatus you have*.) will be gone from MY flat where I let you stay rent-free in MY bed

G *goes*.

F. –

I told you I was mentally ill

E. You did

F. That's really fucking hard

E. I respect you for it

F. Couldn't take two seconds, by the way, I wear the boots bootlickers lick?

E. Didn't get a chance, really, you were straight in with the Loughinisland Was An Inside Job

F. It was an inside job

E. Course it was! They all are

F. And you were sitting there listening, big police head on you

E. I should have led with how many schizophrenics I've killed, should I?

F. I find it so weird and surprising when queer people do violent jobs but I shouldn't

E. At least you know you're patronising

F. –

I wouldn't have fucked you if I'd known what you did

E. That's what, a violation, is it?

F. Didn't say that

E. Good, because last I checked it's a job not an STD, and maybe if you cared that much you should have asked

F. Didn't ask, didn't tell?

E. I like you

F. Boke

E. This was compassionate, I don't want you to make things harder for yourself

F. That's me doing that, is it?

E. New city, could be a new start

F. What makes you think I need a new start?

E. Everything? But, look, I aksh Do Not Give A Shit you had an
episode once, basically all the queers I know are fucking crazy,
but the politics, they're, the yelling racist at people, the weird
photos and the going on about the RUC and the Holocaust to a
half-Jewish officer, / that's just, I don't even know,

F. I didn't know /

E. You could have, if you shut up a fucking second, but all that's
not politics, that's you wanting to feel in control because you're
smarter than everyone else. But you're not, smarter or in control,
no one is, stuff just happens, so do you a deal, take it easy with
the terrorist photography and the harassing my colleagues and
we can go for a pint or two, I'll show you around, help you
make friends, keep you from getting in trouble, see if anything
else happens with us. Because I like you, I do. And I don't want
to play the spooky Nordy, I joined up partly because there's
been way too much of that, but it's different here, and you act
like you understand but you don't, and I worry that someone
who'd refuse to give the Gardaí an alibi for their dad's death on
Principle is going to land themselves in a big mess, way bigger
than being held overnight.

F. –

    I didn't tell you about my dad

E. Yeah you did

F. Don't tell me what happened, I Know

E. If you say so

F. I mean it, don't fucking do that, how did you find out?

E. I rang up my uncle who's a Rothschild and asked

F. Ha ha

E. Got the New World Order on the case

F. Ha fucking ha

E. Does it matter?

F. How you got my file?

E. Fancy yourself much? Like there's a File

F. Or did you phone the Gardaí?

E. You've been here six months, love, the queers can tell me more about you than your paper trail by now, / and that's not even a joke

F. Or was it when I got the vaccine? My details get logged, cross-referenced, something pings for you all down the station?

E. Christ, all joking aside tell me you're not all, fucking – [crackpot? scamdemic?]

F. All what?

E. Microchips in the masks, mercury in the vaccines –

F. Microchips and mercury no, but would the Tories boot people whose visas have expired? Would people I know be scared to get the vaccine because why do they need a National Insurance Number anyway?

E. Got names for me?

F. Not fucking funny you fucking cunt, did you ring the Gardaí? Or the hospital? Oh we know Confidentiality but she's a major suspect in the extremely high-profile case of Who Caught The Racists Rapid Intimidating A Kid / While Touching Their Very Hard Dicks?

E. They got a call about a bunch of kids smashing and grabbing in an offie, they're nearby and see a kid running, / is that That wild?

F. One kid, one kid running, fucking Skipping, and she's wearing shorts, teeny shorts, that matches your profile of a shoplifter, does it

E. Sometimes people fuck up, there's nothing deeper going on there

F. Do you actually believe that? Look me in the eye and tell me you believe there are no racist police in Northern Ireland, / that Every stop is – [justified?]

E. I googled you, I googled you and the first thing that came up was an essay you wrote about it, that's how I know about your dad, I googled you like a big fucking creep.

–

We, [I] hate saying 'we' like The Force or, but We don't give a shit about you, love. Don't flatter yourself. This is all me. I'm trying to do you a favour. Fuck me. I didn't lie to you, I wasn't Under Cover when I came over, I'm not On Surveillance now, I googled you to see what your deal was.

E. –

F. What's your name?

E. You know my name

F. But your second name

E. So you can google me back?

F. Maybe, what's the big deal if I do?

E. Maybe I don't want you to

F. If you don't want to tell me you don't have to, and then I just won't know, lucky you

–

I forgot I wrote that essay, because that whole year is just, my brain was on fire. Hard to remember. But I wrote it because everyone knew, I was supposed to be flying to England that night but then oops, no, you're still here, no week to settle into the apartment before term, stay at home and deal with your headless dad instead, and I hated everyone knowing or thinking they knew without me telling them. So I told my side, even the ugly bit, the asking myself *was the timing deliberate? Was it to stop me leaving?,* to see if that would make it any easier, but mostly no, and that's before My head, or She, and you know, I couldn't tell you which happened first? Did I go see that movie and lose my mind, and then my mother died, or did my mother die and then I lost my mind? I don't know what caused what or if any of it caused any of it, and I could ask her (G.) but that'd just Prove I can't be on my own, and either way He definitely died first so even if I was in hospital already when she died she can say that Him dying is what Set Me Off, so, no escape really, people disagree on What fucked my brain but not If my brain is fucked, and no one cares that I don't feel fucked as long as I'm careful.

(*Answering* E*'s we don't give a shit about you*.) I don't think anyone 'Cares'. I'm not, I know there isn't a Conspiracy. I know no one is In Control. I know I'm not Being Watched. I know you didn't Trick me. I'm Not paranoid, I just hate that there's all these, I hate feeling like people can look at me and I can't look back, like they can just see or think all these things I don't want them to see or think, like wouldn't it be fairer and better and beautiful if Everything was just Out There for everyone so we could all make sense of all of us all at once and forever, and no one would be hurt because they were misunderstood, and maybe I should lead by example. So I wrote that essay. Got paid fifty quid for it too.

E. It was worth more.

F. Thanks.

E. –

What's that?

F. It's for making lissajous figures

E. Yeah?

F. Do you know what those are?

E. No

F *readies a demonstration.* I *enters, still clothed as* I. E *addresses them as though Isaac is their partner.*

I. All good?

E. Just finishing up

F. Ready?

E. Ready

F (*to* I). Ready?

I. For what?

E. Just go

G. You okay?

F. Yeah, I – [am fine? Think so?]

F *does their demo, to general approval.*

E. That's wild

F. My favourite thing to show people

E. Fair

I. Sublime

F. Proof there's a God

G. Fuck's sake

E. Steady on

I. I see it

F (*to* E). No?

E (*to* F). Seriously?

I (*to* E). No?

F. Just look

E (*to* F). Yeah, but proof of God?

I (*to* E). Yeah?

F. Isn't it hard, looking at this, isn't it harder almost to believe it's
not all connected?

E. –

It's fucking cool, anyway

I. For sure

E. Who, would you say invented? Discovered?

F. How to do it?

I. Well the pattern is called a Lissajous curve after a French guy in
the nineteenth century who wanted to make sound visible, which
he did by bouncing a ray of light off two tuning forks at right
angles to one another, and it turned out that when you do that
the light does this, and then it turned out that these patterns also
turn up in space where a planet or a moon or a comet is orbiting
a Lagrangian point of a three-body system, because these curves
are actually graphs of Complex Harmonic Motion and real-life
systems are subject to the amplificative and dissipative forces
that were left out of the mathematical description of Simple
Harmonic Motion by Robert Hooke – (*Spits.*)

F. –

Right

E (*to* I). You're mad into all this, are you?

Sound design builds and we melt from real(ish) time into:

Isaac Ending

As we're taking off into a more abstract/heightened/weird space, this text can all be musicalised in the preaching/psalmodising way that was used earlier.

I. Sixteen hundreds, Robert Hooke – (*Spits.*) plays with springs, makes clocks, sees patterns in flour on a glass plate when he runs a violin bow down its edge.

Sixteen hundreds, I gave a precise mathematical description of how gravity worked but said nothing about how or why because that's God's work.

It's interesting to think.

Full stop.

But it's interesting to think in particular that hallucinations were what were called positive symptoms of what was called schizophrenia, even back in the bad old days

Because they're a presence not an absence

Because they're perceiving meaning where there might not be any, which is unhealthy, instead of not seeing meaning where there's shitloads, which is healthy

Like in the seventeen hundreds, French citizens destroy optical telegraphs because the messages might be royalist

Eighteen hundreds, their great-great-grandmother is born into hunger which epigenetically suppresses a gene implicated in the growth of the cerebellum

Nineteen hundreds, a woman tries to send a bowl of sauerkraut by wire

World War One, soldiers hear Morse messages in gunfire

World War Two, Kurt Godel has an erotic dream about Alan Turing – sweet darling baby angel – and Isaac Newton – aka MOI – getting SAUCY if you know what I mean

The fifties, the first antipsychotics give patients tardive dyskinesia, meaning you can spot them a mile off by the tics, the waving, the grimacing, the blinking, the tongue sticking out

The sixties, their grandmother slices open her hand installing a state-of-the-art toploader washing machine

Their mother runs into a kitchen and slips in a pool of her mother's blood and falls and bangs her head

Their grandmother is worried she'll never recover

At this point, I's voice 'splits' and is doubled by a voice-over – possibly also projected. The double is in bold.

She never recovers /

She recovers

Nineteen seventies, Kurt Godel starves to death to thwart the people trying to poison him to death /

Kurt Godel fears being poisoned so much he chooses to starve instead

Two thousands, computer scientists hide secrets with lava lamps /

Two thousands, eggs are closed

Two thousand eleven, my good friend Steve Jobs dies of cancer /

Two thousand eleven, my good friend Steve Jobs transcends this plane

At this point, I's voice splits again, or (as in our production) is joined by the prerecorded voices of E/F/G – three strands in play now:

Two thousand sixteen, their mother dies in an accident /

Two thousand sixteen, their mother dies by suicide /

Two thousand sixteen, their mother is murdered by people who know how to make it look like an accident

I's voice splits into four now.

Nineteen ninety, the British government burns down the RUC archive /

Nineteen ninety, the RUC archive burns down due to an electrical fault /

Nineteen ninety, IRA members in a false flag op burn down the RUC archive to make the British government look bad /

Nineteen ninety, MI6 officers in a false flag op dressed as IRA members in a false flag op burn down the RUC archive to make the IRA look bad

Two thousand sixteen, they experience the onset of congenital schizophrenia which never remits /

Two thousand sixteen, they experience an idiopathic psychotic episode which never recurs /

Two thousand sixteen, they hear the gods /

Two thousand sixteen, they hear Uchida play Mozart

I's voice splits into eight

Two thousand sixteen, their mother dies shortly BEFORE they drop out of Cambridge /

Two thousand sixteen, their mother dies shortly AFTER she drops out of Cambridge /

Two thousand sixteen, their mother dies shortly BEFORE she drops out of Cambridge /

Two thousand sixteen, their mother dies shortly AFTER she drops out of Cambridge /

Two thousand sixteen, their mother dies shortly BEFORE she drops out of Cambridge /

Two thousand sixteen, their mother dies shortly AFTER she drops out of Cambridge /

Two thousand sixteen, their mother dies shortly BEFORE she drops out of Cambridge /

Two thousand sixteen, their mother dies shortly AFTER she drops out of Cambridge /

Twenty twenties, the British government rounds up the foreigners /

Twenty twenties, public health requires a crackdown on illegal immigrants /

Twenty twenties, there are chips not computer chips like deep-fried potatoes in the vaccines /

Twenty twenties, a man mysteriously dies while being evicted /

Twenty twenties, the Irish police shoot a kid /

Twenty twenties, secret Beyoncé album /

Twenty twenties, the Messiah comes

Twenty twenties, it's not bees

The live I *drops out.*

In the beginning, was the word /

In the beginning, was the bang /

In the beginning, was the word /

In the beginning, was the bang /

In the beginning, was the word /

In the beginning, was the bang /

In the beginning, was the word /

In the beginning, was the bang /

Back to two – I*'s voice and* F*'s voice.*

Always, there was and is and will be a God who loves and understands us /

Always, there was and is and will be a God who loves and understands us

I. Never, will someone who loves you hurt you

Now, it all makes sense at last

Now, we are safe

The End.

Plaintext of F's Speech About Hospital

There was a woman on the ward, bit older than me but beautiful
skin, and I kept thinking aw man, it's such a pity she'd self-harmed,
but she was being really clear with them, she wasn't suicidal, it
hadn't been an attempt, she'd just, you know, Had a Moment, when
she was drunk, and she kept saying I have BPD, I shouldn't be in
this ward, they know me over in Springbank ward, but there's a
nurse who's a prick who kept telling her No Beds In Springbank,
Sweetheart, and she HATES that, understandably, condescending
prick, not that different to the way you only call me sweetheart
when you don't want me to be allowed be angry with you, but that's
what sets her off after a couple of days, he keeps touching her when
he's talking to her, calling her sweetheart, so she hits him, calls him
a fucking creep, and then they isolate her, restraints are illegal now
since the newer Act, can't remember what year, but a door works
just fine when there's someone sitting against the other side, they
wait till she falls asleep in there and carry her out.

HOTHOUSE

Carys D. Coburn
with MALAPROP THEATRE

Introduction

What's all this about?

There's nothing climate breakdown doesn't touch. That means that, in a sense, any story you tell about the world right now is a story about climate breakdown. In another sense no story is, because each speaks inadequately to the full scope of the problem. Climate change is nowhere except everywhere.

So there's a temptation to try and say everything, to have our map be the same size as the territory. But maps are most useful when they bring into focus by shrinking. Zooming out brings more into view, it's true, but seeing more is not the same as understanding more. Waiting forever for the image to finally resolve means the problems never do.

Plus theatre audiences now come pre-deluged in information, which should make us question the deluge's usefulness as a narrative strategy. In the refractory period, further stimulation just irritates. We all know all the punchy soundbites that terrify, about sea level rising A metres by year B, about only X individuals remaining in photogenic species Y by your Zth birthday. Often we are reading about these things when the lights start to dim, and the second the show is over we go back to reading about them. We're all already drowning all the time. We don't need any more more.

What to do? Offer too much truth or not enough? Despair or resignation? Shriek or shrug?

Maybe the only way out is through both those feelings. We can't not feel them but we can work at working with them, at understanding them, at allowing hope – even happiness, who knows? – to exist alongside them. If our grief paralyses, then maybe we need a new grief. Or, if not a new grief entirely, then we at least need to take this grief out and turn it upside down and spin it around and put it back in in a way that leaves space for us to feel something else.

Because sometimes arranging – rearranging – is creating. (There's a nuclear reactor at Oklo in Gabon that nobody built. Uranium and water and enclosed spaces all exist in nature, the 'technology' is all in the pattern between them.) Move your bookshelves to where the couch was and the couch to where the table was and pull the table out, suddenly you can do yoga and host an aftersesh. New stuff can happen. New feelings can be felt. The same things in a new shape are new things.

That's why *HOTHOUSE* is full of jokes and carry-on. There's cabaret numbers from endangered birds, karaoke from a lonely whale, both conga and can-can lines. These gags are not supposed to palliate, *okay the world is ending, but let's have a good time while we still can*! Jolly nihilism is still nihilism, and like all nihilism it's seldom those with the most reason to despair despairing. More often it's those who want to deny the possibility – hence abdicate the responsibility – of change, of changing themselves, who insist things are hopeless and by insisting make it true. We've fucked it! Nothing to be done! We can relax until we die.

That's not how we want people to laugh. The jokes in *HOTHOUSE* are supposed to jolt us in our emotional rut. If you cycle straight down the LUAS tracks, your tyre catches and you smash your face. The only safe way to traverse an entrenched path at your own speed is obliquely. The obliquer, the safer. If we can't cry, it's not enough just to not cry. We have to laugh.

And think about it, if every story is inadequate to the full scope of climate breakdown then so must every feeling be. The sublime apocalypse. The apocalyptic sublime. Laughter is negligibly more inappropriate than sadness. Inviting both, feeling both, rejecting both, we never forget that there's more there to feel more about.

You could think of it like stereopsis; both our eyes see a flat image and because those images diverge, because we can interpret that divergence, we manage to perceive curvature, depth, the fact that there is a surface not currently in view. With two eyes, we can see that there is something we can't see. With two feelings, we can feel that there is something we can't feel.

This is all camp by another name, by the way. We know we didn't invent it but it can feel strange to lay claim to it, speaking on behalf of a bunch of anxious bisexuals. Yes, this is camp, the sensibility that pivots between the meanings of *partial*. Taste is limited because knowledge is limited. If we knew enough we would know how to like everything, but we don't. (The world might be your oyster but oysters are still an acquired taste.) In the meantime, refuting good taste by wallowing in bad taste affirms that the world transcends both. Things are always more than our opinions of them. Maybe all the glitter and eating dogshit and white men in kaftans made it difficult to see, but camp was always about the sublime. (Apocalyptic or otherwise.) It was the secret language of a secret people, and it's a short step from the unspeakable in practice to the unspeakable in principle.

We're not ignoring climate grief by laughing. We're mixing it with something else until it transforms, mixing it lots of different ways so that we see it less and understand it more. Laughing *and* grieving is different from laughing *or* grieving, laughing *then* grieving, grieving *then* laughing, exactly the same way shampooing and conditioning is different from conditioning and shampooing. Emotion is non-commutative. Ordering matters. The same things in a new shape are new things.

Theatre nerds can't stop arguing about what Aristotle meant by *catharsis*. Its root is in *cleansing* or *purging*, but emotion isn't prawns you should have known better than to eat and you can't just vomit it up and feel better. When you stop feeling a feeling, where does it go? Does it die or does it just hide? When it comes back, is it just rerevealed or is it resurrected?

Maybe Aristotle just meant *tidying*. Artists can't make or unmake feelings. The arrogance to think you could! The ignorance of wanting to! There's no LET THERE BE LIGHT. At the very most there's *let there be natural light from that window for the potted plant*. Artists just move feelings around to afford some breathing space, a little gap in which to be someone else who might be a little better off. Arranging – rearranging – is creating.

HOTHOUSE goes to all sorts of times and places, but there's one feeling at the centre of it: wanting to be something else, knowing you need to change, not knowing how. It's a big feeling. It's where we are with the climate. It's where lots of us are with our families too. It's hard to change when you only have role models for everything you want to stop doing. It's scary to change when you want to change into someone you'll have nothing in common with, because isn't that basically the same thing as wanting to stop existing? Is wanting to be someone totally new wanting to die? Assuming it is and remembering everyone has to die at some point in some way, is transforming the worst?

It's not even climate allegory, because feelings don't care what occasion occasioned them. They're always themselves. It doesn't matter whether you're disgusted with the temper you got from your ma or the disposable-coffee-cup habit you got from your da, you're disgusted. It doesn't matter if you're afraid that the permafrost is fucked even if we stop taking Ryanair flights or that your children fear you the way you feared your parents, you're afraid.

It's not even allegory because we're not interested in people having an AH HA moment where they Get It, realise we've been secretly talking about climate breakdown via the family. We'd rather you Get It before you take your seat, spend the show exploring the limits of the mapping for yourself. The comparison is obvious, its entailments and ramifications aren't. If allegory is subtle unsubtlety, secret preachiness, we're aiming for unsubtle subtlety. We're shouting a poem in the hopes that it sticks in your head, that you think about it in a week's time, that you find yourself singing it to the tune of 'thank u, next' in the shower. We're letting you know exactly what we're letting you make up your own mind about.

With a little detachment, it's nearly funny that one of the most popular reactionary mantras on the go is *facts don't care about your feelings*. It would be easy to rebut if the reactionary shitheads actually meant it, and not *I need to believe change is impossible because I'm too scared of disappointment to change or even hope myself*. (Glib nihilism is still nihilism.) Of course facts don't care about feelings, the same way the flu virus doesn't care about your fever. It's not equipped to. It's not its job. This does not mean the fever isn't real. It is. And more, it's real because of the flu! Fever is the body resisting the world changing it. The body tries to change the virus the way the virus changes the body.

Just like that, our feelings exist precisely because of the indifference of factitity. The hard surfaces of the world that bruise us. They're not just a response, they're an alarm. They're a call to do something about it, to do something with it, to change it the way it changes us. To make it softer. The shitheads say *nothing can change*, the fact that we even have feelings says *we can and we have to*.

Our feelings are symptoms of our world. When we talk about them, we talk about it. So let's.

HOTHOUSE was first performed at Project Arts Centre, Dublin, on 9 September 2023, as part of Dublin Fringe Festival. The cast was as follows:

Peter Corboy
Thommas Kane Byrne
Bláithín MacGabhann
Maeve O'Mahony
Ebby O'Toole-Acheampong

Set and Costume Design	Molly O'Cathain
Composition, Musical Direction and Sound	Anna Clock
Associate Sound Designer and Sound Engineer	Eóin Murphy
Lighting Design	John Gunning
Assistant Director	Ellen Buckley
Choreographer	Deirdre Griffin
Costume Supervisor	Mary Sheehan
Stage Manager	Evie McGuinness
Assistant Stage Manager	Dragana Stevanic
Producers	Carla Rogers
	Caoimhe Whelan
Production Manager	Pete Jordan

Originally commissioned by THISISPOPBABY for Where We Live. Supported by the Arts Council / An Chomhairle Ealaíon, with additional support from the field:arts and Project Artists programmes.

Characters

CAPTAIN
FLYCATCHER
GREAT TIT
NURSE
BARBARA
RUTH
DICK
RACHEL
DANIEL
PENROSE
RABBIT
ALI
ROBIN
HARRY
NORA
PARENT
CHILD

Notes on the Dialogue

A forward slash (/) directly after a character prefix indicates that this character speaks the next line of dialogue at the same time as the character named at the beginning of the line. This may include multiple characters speaking in unison.

The play features short extracts from *Silent Spring* by Rachel Carson (first published in the United States in 1962).

This text went to press before the end of rehearsals and so may differ slightly from the play as performed.

Captain One

CAPTAIN. Welcome onboard the *Crystal Prophecy*, this is your captain speaking

I have to say that part

I hate leading with my status

Here are some humanising facts about me for balance

I'm fifty-two, I'm five foot two, and I am extravagantly homosexual

Two lies one truth, you guess which is which!

A clue: I have a husband who I love very much, Raymond

He hasn't replied to my last message, but we're pretty far from everything here, so

ANYWAY

Our latitude is eighty-five degrees, temperature is a balmy ten degrees

Celsius for the Arctic Circle

Oh, and the Meadow Pipit, scientific name *Anthus Pratensis,* just went extinct in the last five minutes

But if everyone is ready for the first of tonight's onboard entertainments, then please adjourn to the ballroom

There you will see a great tit murder a crested flycatcher

Songbird One

A PIED FLYCATCHER *enters. Her black-and-white plumage is handsome. She sings.*

FLYCATCHER. In 1990 my great-great-great-great-great-grandmother

Had sex on April twenty-ninth.

In 1995 my great-great-great-great-grandmother

Had sex on April twenty-eighth.

In the year 2000 my great-great-great-grandmother

Had sex on April twenty-sixth.

In 2005 my great-great-grandmother

Had sex on April twenty-third.

In 2010 my great-grandmother

Had sex on April nineteenth.

In 2015 my grandmother

Had sex on April fourteenth.

In 2020 my mother

Had sex on April eighth.

In 2023 I myself

Had sex on April 1st

And if I'm lucky I'll die when I'm five like them.

A GREAT TIT *enters. Her chest is yellow and fancy. She kills* FLYCATCHER.

TIT. Every year I fuck on the fifth.

April fifth, I fuck on the fifth.

I lay my eggs on April sixth

One day after I fuck on the fifth.

My chicks are born on April nineteenth

Two weeks after I fuck on the fifth.

My chicks fuck off from the nest May tenth

Three weeks after I fuck on the fifth.

Sex in April.

Snow in March.

Sex in April.

Sun in November.

Sex in April again for me.

If I'm lucky I'll die when I'm three.

The Twentieth Century

CAPTAIN. Wasn't that something?

I hope that's prepared you all to get weird, because for our next act I need to take you all the way back to 1969

Last week an American was on the moon

The Hawaiian Honeycreeper, scientific name *akialoa stejnegeri,* has just gone extinct

And in Dublin Fifteen, a postcode where fields are suddenly houses, the nice woman in Connolly Hospital is saying that greenstick fractures –

NURSE. Are very common, both my boys have had them, cast for a couple of weeks and you'll be back to your shenanigans! Hurt herself playing the hoyden, did she? Rough-housing, were we?

BARBARA. Rough-housing

CAPTAIN. Ruth's mother Barbara agrees

She doesn't say much else until they're at home, listening to the Minnie Riperton that's the only record they can both sit still for, Ruth eating the third of three drumstick lollies never normally allowed, and then Barbara says –

BARBARA. He doesn't know his own strength

CAPTAIN. Ruth doesn't know what she's supposed to say to that, so maybe it's a good thing her teeth stuck in the hard lolly mean she keeps her mouth shut

BARBARA. He doesn't know his own strength

CAPTAIN. Is something she says a lot over the years, but in 1969, on the day after nine-year-old Ruth gets her cast, she notices that the level in the one bottle he allows himself at a time has fallen below the label, which means she has to drink it

RUTH *necks whiskey and it burns all the way down and in her nose.*

On the basis that too much for her is better than not enough for him, because it is medically impossible for him to be in a good mood if he can't have

DICK. A proper drink after the day that it's been

CAPTAIN. But he never lets himself finish a bottle and buy one the same night, because

DICK. Everything in moderation

CAPTAIN. And seeing as the pub down the road is, needless to say –

DICK. Common, very common

CAPTAIN. He's a doctor, after all, but given as the pub's out Ruth appreciates the importance of bottles being full or empty only

Empty is okay, despite what you might think, because he gets to say

DICK. The good times must be rolling! Did you see a good time roll past you?

RUTH. No

DICK. WELL CAN YOU DO A TUMBLE LIKE ONE?!

RUTH *attempts a roll with her cast on. It hurts.*

CAPTAIN. He is at his nicest when he can drink as much as he thinks he deserves, if not as much as he wants, and this time is no different

He doesn't say sorry, he never does, but he takes her out looking for rabbits

DICK. Nothing like a lovely rabbit, you'd miss them, when we moved here first it

Was all fields, you could catch rabbits out the back where Jane's house is now, did you know that?

RUTH. No

CAPTAIN. She says, though the truth is –

RUTH. Yes, you've told me before

CAPTAIN. Because he's so happy right now, even if he hasn't said sorry.

DICK. It's getting more and more like the city, more houses, more pylons, more roads, no more rabbits. Some mornings I'm not waking up for work because I'm not hearing the birds any more

CAPTAIN. This is a real reason, but it's one of many.

DICK. It's the DDT, they spray it on all the plants to kill pests but it kills all the birds who eat the pests and all the rabbits who eat the plants too. Might not be any birds in fifty years. Or rabbits. Did I give you Silent Spring?

RUTH. No

CAPTAIN. She says, and means it.

DICK. Great book. Great book. Great book.

CAPTAIN. He says, three times, in the way that means he's forgotten what's going on.

DICK (*in an intense whisper*). LOOK.

CAPTAIN. Please welcome to the stage Madame Rabbit

They see a RABBIT. *They watch, spellbound, as it rabbits around. The* RABBIT *notices them and turns to speak to us. There is music.*

RABBIT. It'd be nice to think our kids will always be better off than us

That they'll grow up to be doctors in the TB hospital where our parents were patients

But I'm a great-great-great-great-grandmother who grew up happy

And my great-great-great-great-grandkids all ate DDT and died

Maybe we see clearest here in Dublin 15, the one generation between tenements and tenements who got back gardens AND front rooms AND condoms AND winters and a shopping centre, even if it took twenty fucking years

Maybe we knew best that progress wasn't

That the changes would change

That the only way to never die is to be already dead

DICK. Will we try catch her?

CAPTAIN. And though Ruth knows he wants her to say –

RUTH. Yes!

CAPTAIN. She says –

RUTH. No.

DICK. No?

RUTH. No.

CAPTAIN. But it's okay, this time, because all he says is –

DICK. I suppose you've just had your supper, it'd be a waste.

The RABBIT *exits.*

CAPTAIN. Madame Rabbit, everyone

Walking home, her father says –

DICK. We'd nothing, growing up, no electricity, toilet out the back, and under rationing if my da came back from the docks with a rabbit, they used to sell them down there, the lads from out here, they'd cycle in with them, but if he got one off them it was a party. He'd take it out from under his coat, you'd to hide them, this is under rationing, but he'd come in the door all hunched and he'd take it out and say look what I found! And we'd be wild. And I didn't brush my teeth until I started going to dances, did I tell you that before

RUTH. No

CAPTAIN. Yes

DICK. And no shoes in summer, did I tell you that?

RUTH. No.

CAPTAIN. Yes.

DICK. And look, you'll probably have a car when you're grown up, and your children'll probably have aeroplanes, and their children will probably have ROCKETS, and what will their children have do you think?

RUTH. I don't know.

DICK. You don't know?

RUTH. No

CAPTAIN. She says, which spoils the game, even though she wants to say –

RUTH. They won't NEED rockets, because they'll LIVE on the moon, and the moon is small.

CAPTAIN. Which she thinks would make him laugh, but doesn't say in case it doesn't. She's so scared to spoil it she spoils it. But it's okay, because a week later there's a parcel on her bed.

RUTH *unwraps a copy of* Silent Spring.

DICK. It's for adults, but you're a clever girl.

CAPTAIN. He says from the doorway where he always stands when he's being nice, ready to run if there are all at once too many feelings.

RUTH. Thank you.

CAPTAIN. She says, already meaning it, before she even knows she will adore this book.

RUTH (*reading*). 'Have we fallen into a mesmerised state that makes us accept as inevitable the inferior or detrimental?'

CAPTAIN. Whenever her mother was screaming, she'd read it

BARBARA (*muffled screaming*).

RUTH. 'Such thinking idealises life with only its head out of water'

CAPTAIN. Whenever her father was roaring, she'd read it

DICK (*muffled roaring*).

RUTH. 'Inches above the limits of toleration of the corruption of its own environment'

CAPTAIN. The one time the Gardaí banged on the door because Mrs Penrose couldn't take any more of it, in 1971 when the St Lucia Wren, scientific name *Troglodytes Aedon* had just gone extinct, that time when Mrs Penrose was genuinely worried someone was being murdered Ruth was reading Rachel Carson's *Silent Spring*

Screaming and roaring and banging on the door, a sudden silence.

RUTH. /

RACHEL. 'Who would want to live in a world which is just not quite fatal?'

CAPTAIN. Please welcome to the stage the one, the only, the Cassandra of Climate Catastrophe, Rachel Carson

RACHEL. Oh stop, you're a dear, quick question, darling

CAPTAIN. Yes, darling?

RACHEL. Why am I here?

CAPTAIN. Because some nights Ruth falls asleep and dreams that you, the author Rachel Carson, are her mother

RACHEL. How sweet!

CAPTAIN. That you live in a forest full of birds that every dawn you scream along with

RACHEL. How charming!

CAPTAIN. That no one ever hits you no matter how loud you are

RUTH and RACHEL scream along with the dawn chorus. No one hits them. This makes them giddy.

RACHEL. To quote the Beach Boys, wouldn't it be nice

Is that an anachronism?

CAPTAIN. The least of many!

RACHEL. When this is happening, it's not commonly known that I'm a big fat lesbian.

But if Ruth as a little girl had known, before the world got to her, she would have wanted lesbian mothers

Because she still thinks women being safer in some ways means they're safe full stop

RACHEL *kisses* RUTH *goodnight on the forehead.*

Goodnight, darling

RUTH. Goodnight, Mom

(*Explaining*.) Americans are moms, not mams

CAPTAIN. When Ruth is twenty-eight and has, in her own words, gotten knocked up by the man she let away with not wearing a newly legal condom, even after he unexpectedly asked

DANIEL. Are you sure?

CAPTAIN. And she, not knowing why, said

RUTH. Yes, I'm sure, just, yes

CAPTAIN. But once that has happened, pregnant Ruth paces her mother Barbara's kitchen because sitting is too sore and asks

RUTH. Did you love him?

BARBARA. Sorry?

CAPTAIN. It's nineteen eighty-eight, the Maui 'akepa, scientific name *loxops ochraceus,* has just gone extinct

RUTH. I asked did you love him

BARBARA. What kind of question is that?

RUTH. 'The obligation to endure gives us the right to know'

BARBARA. If I could go back in time and make him buy you that Minnie Riperton LP instead of that bloody book by bloody Rachel Carson –

RUTH. I never liked Minnie Riperton

BARBARA. Are you joking me?

RUTH. She's fucking aural marzipan

BARBARA. She died of breast cancer

RUTH. Then she's fucking aural marzipan with cancer in one marzipan tit, I never liked her, I was just too scared to tell you

BARBARA. To tell me? (*As in, not him.*)

RUTH. Either of you

Did you love him?

BARBARA. Of course I loved him

RUTH. But you were scared of him

BARBARA. What answer is going to make you happy?

RUTH. That you knew how bad it was, that you could have left but you didn't

BARBARA. I did leave

RUTH. Not until it was too late

BARBARA. Because you were grown up?

RUTH. Was that deliberate? Less stuff to pack? Less shopping until you find a job? No need to worry he'll turn up at my school and find us?

BARBARA. It wasn't too late for me

RUTH. How long did you want to and not do it?

BARBARA. Does it matter?

RUTH. A year? Two? The whole time?

BARBARA. And it wasn't deliberate

RUTH. But you wanted to do it sooner

BARBARA. Did I run out the door the first time the thought popped into my head? Obviously not

RUTH. Why obviously?

BARBARA. Because you want to think it's –

I don't know

A blip on the radar

That things'll go back to being normal

That all this isn't

Normal

But if you leave, you have to admit it.

That you need to

That you should have all along

It's easy now, for all of you

RUTH. To leave?

BARBARA. To tell us off, condemn us, all you women's-lib types with your signs and your hot whiskeys and your keeping your jobs and your let's all leave our husbands all the time, if we even have them

RUTH. So what, fuck us for insisting that women are real people too?

BARBARA. Do you really think I think that? That I'm saying I didn't deserve any better than I got? That none of us did?

RUTH. No

BARBARA. Good, because I'm not, I'm just saying it's hard now to remember what it was like

The shame if I left you behind, the struggle if I took you, couldn't go back to teaching because of the marriage bar, remember, and the benefit for deserted wives was nothing, and that's assuming I would have got it with me doing the deserting

All that before thinking about your father, fathers, husbands, men, how they were just these –

You know your grandfather had another family we never knew about?

That I've a sister I've never met?

How'd he pull that off, when he couldn't boil an egg?

Even when they were there, with you, they were somewhere else where the rules were different

They were these –

I don't know, like hurricanes or earthquakes

You couldn't live with them, talk to them, you just coped with them

And maybe you got so used to coping you forgot you didn't have to, that you shouldn't

I know you know that feeling

RUTH. Do I?

BARBARA. How is it I've disappointed you more than him?

RUTH. Did I say that?

BARBARA. Well why are you here settling scores with me if it's not that? Why aren't you over at his?

RUTH. I don't know

BARBARA. There you go

RUTH. There I go what?

BARBARA. It never even occurred to you you could, same way it never occurred to me

You'll laugh, but I spent years imagining him coming home and me saying something to him, something kind

DICK *comes home, and* BARBARA *looks at him. There is a moment of music where* BARBARA'*s words should be.*

And it'd be right, and he'd say something back, something kind.

There is another moment of music where DICK'*s words should be.*

And it'd keep going like that, saying things and saying things and nothing going wrong, all three of us.

RUTH *joins the imagined moment, and there is another moment of music where words should be.*

And maybe I only realised that that would never happen once you'd already left

Because you'd gone, I thought first, but actually because it was never that I wasn't saying the right thing

I wasn't breaking things

Things just were

Broken

CAPTAIN. At this point, twenty-eight-year-old Ruth would love to say something kind to her mother

There is a moment of music where words should be.

She can feel an uncomplicated love struggling to be born, where she says kind things and her mother says kind things back.

There is a moment of music where words should be.

But the habit is too alien to both of them, turning into someone happier feels too much like dying

So they say nothing, they choose to continue to die slowly rather than all at once

There is a moment of silence.

Kindness won't be commonplace until years after Ruth didn't cry at her father's funeral, years after Barbara read the reading Ruth had refused to read

BARBARA. Then I saw a new heaven and a new earth

CAPTAIN. While Ruth sat holding her new daughter Ali who Mrs Penrose from next door had called

PENROSE. A lovely child!

CAPTAIN. Before getting flustered, conscious of how close she'd come to saying

PENROSE. SHE'S A LOVECHILD!

CAPTAIN. It's 1990, Borreo's Cinnamon Teal and the Dusky Seaside Sparrow and the Atitlán Grebe have all just gone extinct - something in the air, I suppose

BARBARA. For the first heaven and the first earth had passed away

CAPTAIN. Everyone, please welcome back to our stage Madame Rabbit and the spectral presence of Ruth's dead father Richard!

DICK. Will we try catch her?

BARBARA. /

RABBIT. And the sea was no more

DICK. It's the DDT

BARBARA. /

RABBIT. Death will be no more

DICK. Might not be any birds in fifty years

BARBARA. /

RABBIT. Mourning and crying and pain will be no more

DICK. Or rabbits

BARBARA. /

RABBIT. For the first things have passed away

DICK. Beautiful silent fields full of dead things

CAPTAIN. Around this point in the reading Ruth realises that her fond memory of hunting rabbits with her father is fond because

RUTH. That was how he nearly apologised for nearly breaking my arm

CAPTAIN. Which spoils it, more than a little, enough that she finds herself thinking

RUTH. I am their child, I will hurt my daughter, I won't mean to but I will, she will hate me like I hate them, I have to be someone new, I don't know how, the best mother I can be is a dead one but I can't even kill myself without fucking her up too, how does anyone cope with mattering this much to anyone, I can't bear it

CAPTAIN. And though she is a grown woman, she feels just as stuck, just as silly, just as powerless to change what really needs to change, as she felt in 1969 when she tried telling herself

RUTH. Everything will be fine if I never ever ever eat pesticides

BARBARA *puts a cheese and lettuce and tomato sandwich in front of* RUTH.

BARBARA. Eat

RUTH. No

BARBARA. Eat

RUTH. No

BARBARA. Eat

RUTH. No

BARBARA. Eat

RUTH. No

BARBARA. Eat

RUTH. No

BARBARA. Eat

RUTH. No

BARBARA. EAT

RUTH. No

BARBARA. EAT

RUTH. No

BARBARA. You'll die if you don't eat

RUTH. I'll die if I do, carrots have lindane and potatoes have BHC and fish has DDD and cigarettes have arsenic and and and listen!

She has found her page in the book.

Carson SAYS 'The common salad bowl may easily present a combination of organic phosphate insecticides,' which is extra-dangerous because some chemicals destroy the chemicals in your body that destroy bad chemicals so you don't even have to eat that much to be poisoned.

BARBARA. Well if it's a choice between dying fast and dying slow then I know which I'd pick.

RUTH. They're BOTH fast.

CAPTAIN. When Ruth's mother is properly old, old enough to think it's everyone else who's confused, she's in the habit of ringing Ruth and continuing the conversation she's been having with the Ruth in her head, and in one of the last of these calls, in 2011 when the Alagoas Foliage-Gleaner, scientific name *philyder novaesi* has just gone extinct, in that call when Ruth picks up Barbara says –

BARBARA. But you know that was a real turning point in it all, I hope you know, and that I didn't, know, he was no saint but I couldn't have known because he'd not done anything like that before.

CAPTAIN. And Ruth, for all she has imagined this conversation a lot, doesn't immediately get it, even though she remembers very clearly him coming home while she was still staring at her poison sandwich and asking –

DICK. What's wrong with you?

CAPTAIN. And though her mother never ever tells on Ruth, this once she says –

BARBARA. She won't eat.

> DICK *looks at* RUTH *for a long moment. All at once he crosses the room and picks up the sandwich and shoves the sandwich into* RUTH*'s mouth, or tries to. Some of it falls to the floor, and he grabs her and pushes her face into it. After a moment,* DICK *falls to the floor alongside his daughter and starts to grub for food.* BARBARA *joins them after a moment.* CAPTAIN *begins to speak over the action so as to transition us into the next bit.*

Songbird Two / Captain

CAPTAIN. Contrary to what you might be thinking, I actually love birds

> Fair enough, with all the – (*Miming murders.*)

> Not bird birds like women birds

> I mean I LOVED my teenage girlfriends, I really did, but men can break my heart in a way that women never –

> And I remember the first time me and this boy from Model UN kissed it was just

> OH, this is what kissing is SUPPOSED to feel like

> Thank you, Chad, for awakening this joy in me

> He wasn't named Chad, he was representing Chad

> I was Belarus

> But the point is, that's why I'm harping on about birds going extinct

> Birds remind me of the joy that my grief springs from, remind me that fighting back is a form of grieving

> It's traditional to invoke the children to inspire change

Give them a world worth inheriting!

And don't get me wrong, I love children

Me and Raymond have talked about how we'd adopt if not for A) my work, B) the dysfunctions of the adoption system, and C) all the spooky creeps who'd call us paedophiles

So I'm not saying we shouldn't give the children a world worth inheriting

I'm just saying, what a low fucking bar

Because so many birds have already gone extinct that the children will never know what they're missing out on

Most adults, even, never think to miss all the birds that have already disappeared, never stop to think about the beautiful songs they don't hear, the flashes of unexpected colour they don't see

And the most generous I can be is that it's hard to notice an absence, but it's not that hard

Is it too much to expect for people to notice if wrens stop singing in the morning because they're extinct?

Goldfinches? Blackbirds? Robins? Thrushes?

I say they all matter

I say why settle for dying slower when we could fight to live well

I say I want to save ALL the birds *I* love for MY sake, because it'll hurt ME if they die

Like how it hurt to see Chad wanking off Guatemala while sitting in Luxembourg's lap, but only because Chad had helped me see I wanted that for myself

The fleeting pain sounded the depths of my enduring capacity for joy

Or like with great tits

I'm sad that they're killing crested flycatchers, because I wish I could just enjoy their beautiful songs

But they're in distress too, remember, because climate change is making flycatchers migrate earlier and earlier and then what have you got, overlapping mating seasons, bad news, like a hen party turning up in the one genuinely beautifully transgressive cruising spot your city has left, the bride asking for a selfie with you while you, you know, have your mouth full, I think hyperaggression is one understandable response there, and stress is another

They're not evil, great tits, they're stressed

Evil isn't a useful word unless we're talking about the situation, because in an evil situation everyone is guilty, everyone is ashamed, everyone is hurt, everyone is angry, so guilt and shame and pain and anger lose all meaning because they lose all power to transform us

And that's why we're here, to transform, to rediscover the love under the weary hurt, to stop worrying we're fucked long enough to want to fuck, because we're tired of being tired of listening to all the *If everyone generated as much carbon dioxide as Irish citizens, the world could only support one billion people!*

All the *that means we should shut the doors, fuck the refugees, even though the population is still lower than it was pre-Famine!!!*

All the *lithium miners displaced by rising sea levels aren't mining, so the global market in electric cars has crashed and the global suicide rate has spiked!!!*

All the, *FUCK, I miss the bees!!!*

All the *A plane has just crashed near Tomsk in Siberia as a result of extreme turbulence, directly related to thermal pollution from a data centre in Svalbard, directly related to a cryptocurrency transaction in which a Dutch teenager bought child-sex-abuse images an Irish man took in Bangkok!!!*

It's all true, but who can bear all that, all the time?

Not me anyway, and probably not you

Which is why we're here, onboard the *Crystal Prophecy*

Ritually enacting the murder of our avian fellow travellers, bearing witness to the deaths we were too late to stop

As we sail to the Arctic Circle to say goodbye to the ice

Maybe a little late, most of the ice is gone, but at least we're doing SOMETHING, right?

I feel confident saying that there is no place in the world with more joy, more magic, more radical potential, than this billion-dollar cruise ship

I didn't become the youngest sea captain in the line's history for the paycheck, not that it hurts

I did it because HERE is where my shamanic journey needs me to be

So let's take a tour

The Twenty-First Century

We are onboard the Crystal Prophecy. ALI *is bundled up, and* ROBIN *is lurking somewhere in the background wearing a crew uniform, carrying a bottle of champagne.*

CAPTAIN. It's now

Or maybe not now, but a year in the future close enough that you imagine it as not too different

Temperature is a balmy eight degrees for the Arctic Circle

Ruth's daughter Ali is looking out over the rail of the foredeck at where the ice isn't

ALI *looks at* ROBIN. ROBIN *looks expectantly back at* ALI, *as though waiting for some obvious response that* ALI *isn't delivering. Eventually, giving up,* ROBIN *says her first line with a wry friendly energy i.e. it's an injoke that* ALI *doesn't pick up on.*

ROBIN. I couldn't help hearing your accent!

ALI *(bewildered having not said anything)*. Earlier?

ROBIN. Just I'm Irish too

ALI. I'm so sorry

ROBIN. What?

ALI. Nothing, I'm just a dickhead who thinks they're funny

Where are you from?

ROBIN. Can you not tell?

ALI. I'm making conversation, have you never had one?

ROBIN. Cork, but I live in Dublin

ALI. Which one?

ROBIN. Sorry?

ALI. Three? Seven? Eight? Fifteen?

ROBIN. Like postcodes?

ALI. Where in Dublin do you live, yeah

ROBIN. Smithfield

ALI. Fancy, which of your parents owns it?

ROBIN. Neither, they're both dead

ALI. I should probably say sorry, shouldn't I?

ROBIN. That's what people normally do

ALI. But are you sick of people saying it, have you started doing
that thing where you say back *why are you sorry, did you kill
them* just to see what happens?

ROBIN. You've lost a parent too then.

ALI. Kind of? Or, no, never knew my dad is all, but my mam's
about to die if that counts?

ROBIN. I feel like if I say I'm sorry you'll take the piss out of me

ALI. I'm being a bit cunty

ROBIN. They left it to me though, my place, so you're not entirely
wrong

ALI. But cunty

ROBIN. Not entirely wrong but cunty, yes

ALI. Flat?

ROBIN. Two bedrooms

ALI. Balcony?

ROBIN. Roof

ALI. Good job

ROBIN. Why?

ALI. Word is in ten years Dublin Seven'll be two foot underwater, April to November, but you'll still be able to punt to wherever it is you'll be working then

ROBIN. I don't know, the thing about citypunting is that your pole keeps getting caught on all the drowned homeless people

ALI. So working from home?

ROBIN. I'm hoping a robot will have taken all the jobs by then

ALI. So sipping champagne on the roof?

ROBIN. That or inviting someone I don't like very much over and overdosing

ALI. Why – [*Do that*] ?

ALI/ROBIN. So they find you.

ALI. Grim.

ROBIN. Haven't you heard? The best days are officially behind us, it's statistics, or, what, physics or maths, that uncontroversial, from now on it's only getting worse for anyone who can't afford to build a diamond skyscraper in New Zealand

ALI. Yeah?

ROBIN. Quick exit makes sense

ALI. If you believe that, why don't you jump over the side now?

ROBIN. Lots of people do! One of the most popular ways, have a few days of fun on a boat and then disappear without a mess, also one of the most popular ways to murder your wife because the police'll think it's, you know

ALI. Yeah?

ROBIN (*not even a pause, a subtle shift in mood/intonation*). The other thing

ALI. Suicide

ROBIN. Yeah

ALI. You weren't saying it

ROBIN. 'Suicide' then

ALI. It's not like it's so shocking that you can't say it

ROBIN. It's in fucking *Titanic*!

ALI. Is that why that guy is always hanging out down here?

ROBIN. Martin?

ALI. If he's the crewmember who's always 'adjusting' his dick, yeah

ROBIN. Yeah, he's suicide watch, you can probably guess what the mean joke is

ALI. No?

ROBIN. You take one look at Martin and you think –

ALI/ROBIN. It could be worse?

ALI. Ouch

ROBIN. Yeah

CAPTAIN. During this pause, down in his room, Martin wanks furiously

   MARTIN *wanks furiously.*

   The porn he is watching is one video on a terabyte hard drive full of them, which he traded Femi four packs of condoms for, because false hope is worse than no hope and neither sucks your dick

   MARTIN *wanks even more furiously.*

   It is only when his momentum has built considerably that he realises there are no women involved in this anal gangbang

   MARTIN *slows to a brief stop*

   Which is a surprise but not a problem

   MARTIN *continues wanking with renewed vigour.*

ALI. Does it flood in winter?

ROBIN. The ship?

ALI. Your building back home.

ROBIN. March the last three years running.

ALI. I suppose they're right then.

ROBIN. That it's all fucked?

ALI. That we're fucked, yeah.

ROBIN. Why are you here if you don't believe it?

ALI. On a climate cruise?

ROBIN. To look at where the ice isn't, yeah.

ALI. I won a competition.

ROBIN. Really?

ALI. Yeah.

ROBIN. Gas.

ALI. Yeah, couldn't afford it otherwise, and wouldn't even if I
    could, obviously, no offence

ROBIN. No offence?

ALI. As in no judgement, we all have to pay the rent, or, the bills
    anyway, but hanging out on the deeply tacky deeply ironic boat,
    Hey, let's burn lots of fucking fossil fuels bringing a lot of rich
    people to the arctic so they can try feel something about the fact
    that their lifestyle is directly responsible for the death of the
    planet, aggressively not my jam

ROBIN. Top up?

ALI. Please

    ROBIN *tops up* ALI*'s champagne flute, but deliberately overfills*
    it with the same wry friendly energy she used to greet ALI *in the*
    first place. ALI *fails to pick up on this, pulling away the flute*
    and getting fizz on herself.

ROBIN (*ostentatious, knowing*). OH NO!

ALI. What the fuck?

ROBIN (*ostentatious, knowing*). I'm a terrible waiter.

ALI. Are you waiting for me to disagree?

ROBIN (*disgruntled that* ALI *isnt playing ball*). Why did you come if you think all this is that gross?

ALI. I didn't ask for this, I didn't pay for it, I didn't feed the market for it, the champagne is free, why not?

ROBIN. So, what, if the person in the cabin next to you falls asleep with a cigarette lit and starts a fire, you're going to refuse to leave your room and burn to death because it's not your fuck up?

ALI. My uncle actually died in a fire

ROBIN. I don't believe you

ALI. Good, that's total bullshit

ALI *downs her champagne flute.*

ROBIN. Top up?

ALI. Do you think I'm an alcoholic?

ROBIN. No

ALI. Because I'm not

ROBIN. Okay

ALI. And I should know, my mother was an alcoholic

ROBIN. Okay

ALI. I'm just trying to have a good time while the free champagne lasts

ROBIN. Are you?

ALI. Am I what?

ROBIN. Having a good time

CAPTAIN. During this pause, the Arctic breeze which doesn't feel arctic, or even Baltic at that, carries a snatch of the conversation sixty-year-old Harry is having on the deck above them with seventy-year-old Norah

HARRY. There it is right there!

NORAH. I don't see it!

HARRY. A little to the left!

NORAH. Oh I see it!

HARRY. The place where there is not any ice!

NORAH. It's so not beautiful!

HARRY. My breath is so not taken!

NORAH. I'm not feeling sad!

HARRY. I'm not feeling any sense of closure!

NORAH. I'm not glad we came!

HARRY. I'm not going to remember this forever!

NORAH. That's true, because we're not going to live forever

HARRY. It's all true

NORAH. Yes.

HARRY. I don't know what I expected to feel

NORAH. I did

HARRY. What?

NORAH. Sorry

HARRY. That it has happened like this?

NORAH. For letting ourselves believe science was neutral, for
    saying true but glib things like *don't overextrapolate current
    trends, it's not like everyone died of AIDS by the millennium*,
    when we knew that half as much carbon and no increase would
    be too much, that methane is worse, that when the permafrost
    melted it would become a feedback loop where the more it
    melts the more it melts, the more it warms the more it warms,
    the more we die the more we die. For joking that *worst-case
    scenario New York is a beautiful forest in a century,* when we
    knew about trophic cascade, when we knew from wolves and
    hyenas and coyotes that no more predators means every other
    population booms and gorges and starves and vanishes, when
    we knew we were a tumour the world couldn't excise without
    bleeding to death

HARRY. And are you?

NORAH. Sorry?

HARRY. Yes

NORAH. No

HARRY. Maybe you should say it anyway

NORAH. Say it?

HARRY. To the ice, to where it used to be.

NORAH. I'm sorry

Pause as they wait to feel something.

HARRY. I was in love with you, you know

NORAH. Even though I was older?

HARRY. Even though

NORAH. I knew

HARRY. And I never did anything about it

NORAH. Buddhists would say that for a feeling to be real, you have to act on it

HARRY. Buddhists would say that not acting is acting

NORAH. What feeling made you not act?

HARRY. Fear

NORAH. Of what?

HARRY. That you knew and telling you would change nothing

NORAH. Telling me would have changed you

ALI *and* ROBIN*'s convo resumes. Maybe it's a new location. Maybe it's continuous.*

ROBIN. Did you have to enter?

ALI. Enter what?

ROBIN. The competition you won to be here, did you put yourself forward for it?

ALI. It was at work

ROBIN. Raffle?

ALI. First to hit a fundraising target

ROBIN. Non-profit?

ALI. Developing world microloan startup for women

ROBIN. Wow!

ALI. Oh we're fucking vampires, don't get me wrong

ROBIN. Shit, really?

ALI. First against the wall, our biggest funder is an American conglomerate that actually does what everybody accuses China of doing

ROBIN. Meaning?

ALI. They get around the ban on land purchases in East Africa by seizing our clients' plots when they default

ROBIN. Do they?

ALI. Default?

ROBIN. Yeah

ALI. Hard not to when flooding fucks your harvest and closes your daughter's college, yeah

ROBIN. Jesus

ALI. Yeah

ROBIN. But you're their best fundraiser

ALI. What?

ROBIN. You won the competition, didn't you?

ALI. Yeah.

ROBIN. Because you're just that good

ALI. No

ROBIN. So you tried extra-hard because of the cruise tickets?

CAPTAIN. During this pause, the kiwi, scientific name *apteryx australis*, goes extinct

ALI. Do you fuck women?

ROBIN. Wow!

ALI. No? because if you don't then, you know, false advertising

ROBIN. Well, go ahead and report me to the sapphic ombudsman

ALI. So you don't?

ROBIN. Did I say that?

ALI. No, but never saying it outright always feels very I Watch *Drag Race* With My Boyfriend to me

ROBIN. I've never had a boyfriend

ALI. Ah ha!

ROBIN. Or just a relationship, even, is the only reason I hesitated, I'm gay but the fucking has mostly been hypothetical

ALI. Aw

ROBIN. Fuck off

ALI. But hypothetically, do you want to?

ROBIN. Sleep with you?

ALI. Fuck me

ROBIN. Why?

ALI. Why not?

ROBIN. So you're gay?

ALI. I identify more as a Libra

ROBIN. Ha fuckin ha

ALI. Does that surprise you?

ROBIN. I wasn't sure if I was getting a vibe from you or not

ALI. This right here is the vibe

CAPTAIN. During this pause, eighty-five-year-old millionaire Jason says to twenty-five-year-old Lisa

JASON. Do you know what's funny?

LISA. What

JASON. The average speed of climate change right now is two and a half metres per day, meaning if YOU'RE a flower growing over there, and what a precious flower you are by the way, you would have to come over here to where I am for your environment NOT to change, and then do it again tomorrow and tomorrow and tomorrow, Macbeth, Shakespeare, forever.

Doesn't that make you want to seize the day? Grasp pleasure with both hands before it disappears? Have a drink with me maybe?

Pause.

You have a transcendent rack by the way

Pause.

I'm a millionaire

LISA. Do you know what's funny?

JASON. What, darling?

LISA. This is the only way I can travel, because I got arrested on purpose at a protest, not even a good one, and do you know what's REALLY funny?

JASON. What?

LISA. I did it even though the fight I really wanted to join was in America, even though they warned me, because on some level I really thought I was going to change it all overnight, or maybe because I was ashamed that I had a choice about getting arrested, that I had never had to worry about clean air or drinking water or birth defects, and do you know what's really REALLY funny?

JASON. What?

LISA. That you don't realise me talking to you is part of my punishment

ALI. So do you lose your job if you fuck passengers or something?

ROBIN. I'm not a crew member.

ALI. Just wearing the uniform for fun?

ROBIN. Wait, is this not roleplay?

ALI. What?

ROBIN. Did you genuinely forget?

ALI. What?

ROBIN. I'm a passenger too, we had dinner together the first night.

ALI. Seriously?

ROBIN. Seriously.

ALI. Shit, really?

ROBIN. Yes, really. Did you really forget?

ALI. So why are you dressed as crew?

ROBIN. They've all been doing it, didn't you notice? To pass the time, because there's so much repetition, all the dancers have been singing, all the singers have been dancing, all the bar staff have been playing music and the string quartet are behind the bar

ALI. Oh

ROBIN. I swapped with Maya, she's twenty-two, saving so she can go to art college in London, just to see would it be less boring, or, not just, I felt bad for her because the creepy millionaire won't leave her alone

ALI. And does it work?

ROBIN. Swapping?

ALI. Are you less bored?

ROBIN. The problem is that no matter who you are, you're still on the fucking boat

ALI. Right

ROBIN. Did you really forget?

ALI. I had a lot to drink

ROBIN. I know, I put you to bed

ALI. You really must think I'm an alcoholic

ROBIN. I think if you have to worry that you are then it's a warning sign

ALI. Then I was an alcoholic at twelve, what did we talk about?

ROBIN. At dinner?

ALI. Did you know all about my work? About my mam? Fuck, did you tell me about your parents already?

ROBIN. No. You mostly just bitched about the other passengers, and how gross this all is

ALI. Like a complete dickhead

ROBIN. I'd love to disagree

ALI. So why did you come talk to me then?

ROBIN. Because I wasn't sure if I was getting a vibe from you or not

CAPTAIN. Coats on, everyone, temperature dropping to minus two or three as night falls

It is with great sorrow I must announce that the African Grey Parrot, scientific name *psittacus erithacus,* has gone extinct

But it's my pleasure to tell you that atmospheric conditions are perfect for the aurora borealis

If you would all like to fall perfectly silent, you may be able to hear the last humpback whale on earth singing, and please forgive any minor errors that may result from all the plastic bags she's swallowed

A whale sings. The aurora borealis breaks out. ALI and ROBIN look at each other a little awkwardly. One makes a move on the other. Things are just starting to be easy/comfortable/passionate when ALI's phone goes off.

ALI. Sorry.

ROBIN. Don't be. Oh, are you – ?

ALI. Going to take it?

ROBIN. Yeah

ALI. I should, with my mam

ROBIN. Sorry, of course, I'll go

ALI. Don't! It's probably nothing

ROBIN. You're sure?

ALI. Please, stay

   ALI *answers the phone.*

CAPTAIN. The voice on Ali's phone says

   Sit down

   Not good

   Bad actually

   Really bad

   For real this time

   Neuropathy

Sepsis

Worse than the disease

Amputation

Woman of her age

Standard of life

Come home

ALI. I can't

CAPTAIN. And the voice says

You need to come home

ALI. I said I can't, I didn't mean I won't

CAPTAIN. And the voice says

Say goodbye

Last chance

Regrets

Making things right

Heat of the moment

Duty

And she says

ALI. I can't, but even if I could come back I wouldn't because what's there to say? To do? I've been expecting this my whole adult life and at this point it's a relief, to be honest, it's a relief to get to stop waiting for it to finally actually happen. It'll be a relief to never have to talk about her oesophegeal varices again, to never rush to the hospital thinking *oh fuck this is really it this time* again, to never clean blood off that fucking chair she loves so fucking much again, to never stand in a fucking Tesco queue in my school uniform trying to hide fucking incontinence pads between boxes of cereals again or get a cup thrown at me when all I was trying to do was keep her from embarrassing herself

CAPTAIN. The voice says nothing

ALI. You tell me how I'm supposed to feel sad, now, after everything

CAPTAIN. The voice says nothing

ALI. I'm not sad, I'm not angry even, I'm just tired, I've felt all I have to feel, I've said all I have to say, I just want it to be over, if I'm anything I'm glad that it finally is

CAPTAIN. The voice says nothing

ALI. I'm glad it's over, that I'm allowed stop trying, if she asks, she won't, but if she asks tell her that

CAPTAIN. And she hangs up

> During this pause, the last polar bear takes the second last off life support

> It's in their will that they'd rather die all at once than slowly.

ROBIN. I have a stupid question

ALI. I'm alright

ROBIN. I don't think that's true

ALI. No, but I meant what I said

ROBIN. Okay

ALI. About not being sad, I'm not

ROBIN. Okay

ALI. Really

ROBIN. Okay!

ALI. You must want to go

ROBIN. Only if you want me to

ALI. Bullshit, you didn't sign up for this

ROBIN. You don't sign up for compassion, it's compulsory

ALI. I have a horrible question though

ROBIN. Okay

ALI. You can go after I ask it if you want to

ROBIN. Okay

ALI. Did your mother ever hit you?

ROBIN. Do you mean when I was small for being bold?

ALI. Or the other way

ROBIN. No

ALI. Which?

ROBIN. I don't know why I asked that, like it depends, the answer is just no

ALI. Do you miss her?

ROBIN. So so much, both of them, because they were beautiful.

ALI (*scarequoting the sincerity if not taking the piss*). 'Beautiful'!

ROBIN (*totally sincere*). Yes, beautiful

ALI. Big word

ROBIN. Yes

ALI. Both supermodels?

ROBIN. You're funny

ALI. Am I?

ROBIN. Just you seem so oblivious and off in your own world / and –

ALI. Self-centred?

ROBIN. I wasn't going to say it, but yes, but you seem all that one minute and then you say something that makes me think you know where all my bruises are and you can press on them any time you like

ALI. Yeah?

ROBIN. Like earlier

ALI. When?

ROBIN. You spooked me when you caught that I wasn't saying suicide, because I wasn't, consciously I mean, because I work in mental-health policy and so I know all about saying *died by* instead of *committed*, and not reporting methods because of copycats, and that ideation is fundamentally an irrational state, which is maybe why using the word feels wrong when I consider it, or when you suggest it, jumping over the side while Celine Dion sings, because they really were beautiful, my parents, and my life has objectively just been worse since they died, they loved me so so much and now no one does.

ALI. –

ROBIN. Oh god, please don't feel pressured into saying you love
me

ALI. I wasn't

ROBIN. No?

ALI. Going to, or even feeling that

ROBIN. Not even a little?

ALI. Not THAT lesbian

ROBIN. Phew!

ALI. It's just a little shocking to hear

ROBIN. Is it that rare? Or do people just not like to say 'no one
loves me'?

Or think it, even? I've thought about it a lot, since, if too much
is worse than not enough, because then enough never feels like
enough?

But I don't say the word because it doesn't feel irrational, it feels
like jumping or hanging or bleeding out in a bath is a rational
response to it only getting darker from now on, and you saw that

ALI. I actually didn't, I was just trying to make you uncomfortable

ROBIN. And it did! You didn't know what you were seeing, but
you saw it

ALI. I'm her daughter

ROBIN. Yeah?

ALI. She was the same, always had a weapon to hand

ROBIN. And she – ?

ALI. Yeah?

ROBIN. Going back to your question

ALI. Hit me?

ROBIN. Wasn't that what you were saying?

ALI. No, actually, and she was really proud of that

ROBIN. Proud?

ALI. She'd always say it after she'd thrown something at me, or broken something I liked, or pinched me

ROBIN. Pinched you?

ALI. Pinching didn't count as hitting unless she broke the skin, which she mostly didn't once I got big enough to fight back

ROBIN. Oh

ALI. And to be fair to her, she never meant to she just

ALI/RUTH. Didn't know her own strength.

ALI. AND she mostly left me alone after the time I knocked her down the stairs, it was an accident but still, don't feel great about that, easily the worst thing we ever did to each other

ROBIN. But was that when you were a kid?

ALI. Teenager, I think, old enough to know better anyway

ROBIN. And she wasn't?

ALI. I don't need you to make it okay, I'm just trying to explain what it was like

ROBIN. Okay

ALI. My point was, if it was kicking off she'd start in about

ALI/RUTH. We can do it the hard way if you want, I know ALL ABOUT the hard way, I have fucking STITCHES from my dad, we can DO fucking STITCHES if you want

ALI. And when I graduated college she said

ALI/RUTH. You made it, you're finished, I'm off the clock and you're off into the world and no one's broken your heart

ALI. And THAT broke my heart, that stupid fucking joke, that she thought because she was only half as fucked up as her fucked up parents, only half as alcoholic as her alcoholic dad, she wa- fine

CAPTAIN. During this pause, Ruth in hospital in Ireland, lets herself press the button to call the nurse she had wanted to press an hour ago, finally ready to admit that pain hurts and morphine might not be the worst idea

ALI. I'm not her but I'm not nice

ROBIN. Don't say that

ALI. I'm sorry I took the piss out of you

ROBIN. When?

ALI. Don't pretend it's fine

ROBIN. I'm not, I meant like which time

ALI. Fuck sake, of course, I meant the sapphic ombudsman and all that

ROBIN. You meant when you took the piss out of me for being a fake queer and a virgin

ALI. Yeah

ROBIN. That's okay, you're not the first and won't be the last

ALI. To have an unfounded dyke superiority complex?

ROBIN. Are they ever?

ALI. Founded?

ROBIN. Yeah

ALI. No

ROBIN. But being weird and mean about me not having sex was what I meant

ALI. I do the same thing she did, I go around all what's the big deal, I could be meaner than this instead of just not being mean

And I even drink too much too, less than her but too much

ROBIN. You're not her

ALI. No, but I don't know how to not be like her

I don't know how to be something new that won't hurt

CAPTAIN. Hi, everyone, this is your captain speaking

Before I say what I have to say, I need to say this:

However much this sounds like a joke, it isn't

Even though there are like eleven reasons that it does

Sound like one, I mean

A joke, I mean

You get me

Anyway

We have hit an iceberg

I know

And we are sinking

And I'm not going to sugarcoat this, all our communications are out

Because this is the last cruise, so the company said *WHY BOTHER REPLACING THE COMS FOR THE LAST CRUISE, WHAT ARE THE CHANCES THERE'LL BE A DISASTER ON THE VERY LAST TRIP?!*

WHY REPLACE THEM IF THEY'RE JUST GOING TO FRY AGAIN?

Oh god, Raymond, I don't think I ever made you understand how much I fucking love you

Loved

The irony being we thought the last cruise was the last cruise, if you get me

I'm not going to lie, I've been drinking

As in, the one before this

And the one before that, and the one before that, basically we thought it would all be over five years ago, but then the ice went and people kept booking, so we just kept doing the tours to visit where the ice USED to be

And the radio has been broken the whole time

We never fixed something that was so easy to fix because we thought the end was in sight

The only reason it matters is because we thought it didn't

So yeah, we're sinking and no one is going to save us and we're all going to die

Just keep doing what you're doing

There's no reason not to

A long moment where ALI *and* ROBIN *look at each other.*

Then they begin to make love as the ship sinks.

Possibly this section bleeds into Songbird Three, with the quintet beginning one voice at a time.

Songbird Three

A barbershop quintet of birds sing.

SONGBIRDS. The whales are gone

The wolves are gone
The bears have slipped away
No robins sing
No sparrows sing
To mourn the broken day.

No great tits sing
No chaffinches
No pigeons and no crows
No cassowaries
Ostriches
Penguins herons ravens doves

Swallows magpies cardinals
Parrots gannets gulls
For the first time in sixty million years
Silent climbs the sun.

The Twenty-Second Century

There can be one parent or many.

CAPTAIN. It's the next century

Picture houses you would struggle to call houses, and zoom in on one at the heart of the cluster

Its walls are made of something you've never seen

It has a central courtyard with an ancient tree

The house was built around it, it was here first

Forty people live here, but most aren't in right now

Inside the house there are parents who have a child, that's not me fucking up my lines and saying the nouns in the wrong order, this is a world where not all parents have children

The child isn't an orphan, basically, the opposite in fact

They'd call all of us orphans, at that

They are speaking a language that doesn't exist yet

It sounds like every English except the English English people speak

If you don't speak it yourself then listening to it spoken is quite like sharing a hostel room with Dutch people on a moderate quantity of shrooms, so we'll spare you that

You're on the shrooms, not the Dutch people

The child and their parents are learning about each other, which we call small talk, or playing a game, which we call getting an education

They have one word for both those things, but it's hard to pronounce

PARENT. When you read old books, parent means someone who has a child

CHILD. True

PARENT. Parents look after each other

CHILD. True

PARENT. Every parent has parents

CHILD. True

PARENT. Rivers are parents

CHILD. True

PARENT. Trees are parents

CHILD. False, but forests are

PARENT. True, when every parent parents every parent everything works

CHILD. True

PARENT. Two parents can have a child but two parents shouldn't raise a child

CHILD. True, at least three

PARENT. Parents per child?

CHILD. Yeah

PARENT. True, and there's nine kids in our house so we're pretty normal

CHILD. True

PARENT. For most of history parent wasn't a real job

CHILD. False

PARENT. For most of history parent wasn't a money job

CHILD. True

PARENT. Parent is the only real job

CHILD. False

PARENT. False?

CHILD. Putting out fires

PARENT. True, putting out fires is really important, but if you think about it that's parenting trees

CHILD. True, and the deer who live in the trees

PARENT. False, deer don't live in the trees

CHILD. AMONGST

PARENT. I wanted to birth for my first five-year but I also wanted to travel, so your parent birthed you for THEIR first five-year and now I'm your big parent while THEY travel

CHILD. My blood parent?

PARENT. Yeah

CHILD. True, and my other blood parent is a doctor on the other side of the continent

PARENT. True, and you can take the long train to visit them when you're a bit older

CHILD. True, and I'll do that instead of birthing

PARENT. Yeah?

CHILD. Yeah

PARENT. Can I come with you?

CHILD. We'll see

PARENT. Okay then

CHILD. And my birth parent is doing a ten-year

PARENT. True, which is very impressive

CHILD. True, and they're studying germs

PARENT. Germs?

CHILD. Germs

PARENT. True, I guess, they're studying horizontal gene transfer

CHILD. True, in germs

PARENT. True, because what we choose isn't just about what's good for us, it's about what's good for the next seven generations

CHILD. True

PARENT. And there might not be seven generations after them, but that doesn't change much for us

CHILD. True

PARENT. And in a million years there might be a germ that can eat the plastic in our bones, so we shouldn't worry too much about leaving our individual mark

CHILD. False

PARENT. False?

CHILD. I AM THAT GERM

PARENT. Oh YOU'RE that germ, okay, and you're eating my bones, significantly ahead of schedule, thank you, you're so gracious

CHILD. True, and you're my favourite parent

PARENT. Yeah?

CHILD. Yeah

PARENT. That's nice to know

CHILD. You knew already

PARENT. And you're allowed change your mind about who's your favourite

CHILD. True, but I won't

PARENT. False

CHILD. True

PARENT. You won't change your mind ever?

CHILD. No

PARENT. False

CHILD. I won't change my mind much

PARENT. You're allowed to if you want

CHILD. True, but I don't

PARENT. True, I suppose

My favourite food is rabbit

CHILD. True, but my parent hates it

PARENT. True, and no one eats salmon

CHILD. True, because they need to recover

PARENT. True, because we ate so many

CHILD. True, and they bring nitrogen to forests

PARENT. False, fish don't live in forests

CHILD. False, bears eat fish and do shits in forests

PARENT. True, one hundred years ago there were a lot more people

CHILD. True

PARENT. The problem was never too many people

CHILD. True

PARENT. It took violence to make the big changes happen

CHILD. False

PARENT. False?

CHILD. It took violence to keep things the same

PARENT. Your parent told you to say that

CHILD. True, but that doesn't mean it's NOT true

PARENT. True

CHILD. And those people could have just stopped

PARENT. True, but they didn't

CHILD. True, so they got blown up

PARENT. False

CHILD. Some of them got blown up

PARENT. True, but before they got blown up your great-grandparent was stuck on a sinking ship in the Arctic

CHILD. True

PARENT. And she thought it was hopeless

CHILD. True

PARENT. In every rational sense of the word, it was in fact hopeless

CHILD. What does rational mean?

PARENT. Profit-oriented

CHILD. What does THAT mean?

PARENT. Acting as though human dignity is best cultivated by the pursuit of economic surplus, even though economic surplus by definition requires the immiseration of labour

CHILD. Those aren't real words

PARENT. True, I just meant no matter how she looked at things it looked hopeless

CHILD. True

PARENT. And then a penguin swam up to the side of the ship and said

PENGUIN. *Hey you party people, our pals Greta Thunberg and Mary Robinson mentioned you might need some help right about now*

PARENT. And your great-grandparent said

ALI. *What the fuck*

PARENT. And the penguin said

PENGUIN. *Legit, believe, famslice, big first woman president energy*

CHILD. Because that was how they talked a hundred years ago

PARENT. Just penguins or everyone?

CHILD. Yep

PARENT. Which?

CHILD. I said YEP

PARENT. True, and then the captain of the ship said

CAPTAIN. *Can you save us?*

PARENT. And the penguin said

PENGUIN. *You know it, babe, hop into the water*

CHILD. And my great-grandparent said

ALI. *We'll freeze to death if we do that*

PARENT. And your blood great-grandparent said

ROBIN. *We'll freeze to death if we stay here too*

CHILD. And the penguin said

PENGUIN. *Trust us, life won't go out, I can't tell you how but I can feel the way that I can't see*

PARENT. And the captain of the ship said

CAPTAIN. *Okay, I trust you, but if I die make sure Raymond knows I love him*

CHILD. AND HE JUMPED

PARENT. True, and he SCREAMED because the water was so cold

CHILD. True, and the penguin pinched his nose in its beak

PARENT. True, and the penguin pulled him off by the nose to Svalbard

PARENT. /

CHILD (*because he's being pulled by the nose*). AAAAAAAAAAAAAAAAAAAAAAAH

CHILD. Which is a very cold island full of plants all over

PARENT. True, and when the captain got there he lay on the plants all over and cried he was so glad to be alive

CHILD. True, but that wasn't for a while yet because Svalbard was far away

PARENT. True, and back at the ship your great-grandparent was the next person to jump

CHILD. FALSE

PARENT. False?

CHILD. My great-grandparent was last, and my blood great-grandparent was second last

PARENT. True, and your great-grandparent said

ROBIN. *Everyone else is jumping*

CHILD. True, and my great-grandparent said

ALI. *I know we should but I'm scared*

PARENT. And then?

CHILD. THEY HAD A BIG SMOOCH ON A SINKING SHIP

PARENT. True, and then your blood great-grandparent jumped

CHILD. True, and she said

ROBIN. *Fuck*

PARENT. And then your great-grandparent jumped

CHILD. True, and she said

ALI. *Fuck fuck fuck*

CHILD. True, and penguins pinched their noses in their beaks

PARENT. True, and pulled them off by the noses to SVALBARD

PARENT. /

CHILD. /

ALI. /

ROBIN. AAAAAAAAAAAAAAAAAAAAAAAAAH

CHILD. And when they got to Svalbard they lay on the plants all over and cried they were so glad to be alive

PARENT. True, and they all lived happily ever after

CHILD. False

PARENT. FALSE?!

CHILD. Because they were at the NORTH pole and the NORTH pole had BEARS, not PENGUINS!!!!!

PARENT. Very good / True, there were bears not penguins but everyone did live happily ever after

CHILD. False

PARENT. False?

CHILD. Because there's floods and plagues still

PARENT. True, and there's still fights, but not wars, and still hunger, but not famine

CHILD. It's hard to say

PARENT. Yeah?

CHILD. Yeah. Another.

PARENT. Another?

CHILD. Another hard one

PARENT. A hard one?

CHILD. A REALLY hard one

PARENT. A REALLY REALLY hard one?

CHILD. Like, a snail

PARENT. What?

CHILD. As hard as a snail

PARENT. But snails are soft!

CHILD. THEIR SHELLS

PARENT. Okay then, a really really hard one like a snail, let's see, you ready?

CHILD. Yeah

PARENT. YOU SURE?!

CHILD. YEAH

PARENT. Okay, well, there is no redemption for us in outgrowing the past, the wounds we pushed into our own flesh on the points of its teeth as we crawled out of its clenched mouth into somewhere more free will never heal, there is no hope, no glory, no transcendence in ceasing to be defined by our pain, *I scream therefore I am* or *I am therefore I scream*, no triumph in being more than a wound because we always should have been more, there is only an aching joy for those who will grow up not having to remember, joy that they will never love anyone the way we love them, joy that love as they love will always feel pale to us but will never scald them

CHILD. False

PARENT. Yeah?

CHILD. Those aren't real words so they don't MEAN anything real

PARENT. And tell me this, you clever small person, what is a REAL word?

CHILD. That people know

PARENT. And you are people

CHILD. True, and you're crying

PARENT. True

CHILD. Because of what you were talking about

PARENT. True

CHILD. Why?

PARENT. You wouldn't understand

CHILD. False

PARENT. True

CHILD. False

PARENT. True

CHILD. False

PARENT. True

CHILD. False

PARENT. I don't want you to understand

CHILD. True

The End.

Company Biographies

CLAIRE O'REILLY

Claire is an Irish theatre director with a primary focus on new work. Upcoming projects include MALAPROP's *HOTHOUSE* by Carys D. Coburn (Dublin Fringe 2023), *This Solution* by Shaun Dunne (Dublin Theatre Festival 2023) and *Talking Round the Fire* by Chris Thorpe (Royal Court 2023). Recent projects include *Bulrusher* by Eisa Davis (The Lir Academy 2023), *A Family Business* by Chris Thorpe (Staatstheater Mainz 2022), *Accents* by Emmet Kirwan (Dublin Fringe 2022), and *Christine* by Jennifer Jonson (Peacock Theatre Dublin 2022). Associate director credits include *A Streetcar Named Desire* (dir. Rebecca Frecknall, Phoenix Theatre 2023), *Dr. Semmelweis* (dir. Tom Morris, Harold Pinter Theatre 2023). Assistant director credits include *Uncle Vanya* (Sonia Friedman Productions 2020) and *Translations* (Royal National Theatre 2019), both dir. Ian Rickson. Claire is a former Resident Director at the Abbey Theatre (2022–23). She has a Masters in Drama Directing from the Bristol Old Vic Theatre School (2019) and is a graduate of Film and Theatre at Trinity College Dublin (2015). She is currently developing a drama for young people for RTÉ.

CARYS D. COBURN

Carys D. Coburn was the winner of the Verity Bargate Award 2017 for *Citysong* – co-produced by Soho Theatre, the Abbey Theatre, and Galway International Arts Festival. Other plays include *Boys and Girls* (Best New Writing Award Dublin Fringe 2013, Stewart Parker Trust Award nominated); *Drawing Crosses on a Dusty Windowpane* (Dublin Fringe 2015); *BlackCatfishMusketeer* (Dublin Fringe 2016, subsequent UK and Chinese tours), and *Absent the Wrong* (Best Production at Dublin Fringe 2022).

Short work includes *Me, Sara* for the Abbey's Priming the Canon; *ALASIALIAS* for Paines Plough's *Come To Where I'm From* and *Our Mother, My Daughters* for Draíocht Blanchardstown's

HOME Theatre. Work with young people is a major strand of their practice; they are the author of *Ask Too Much of Me* for the NYT ensemble (Peacock Theatre 2019); *this is a room...*, for Dublin Youth Theatre (Dublin Theatre Festival 2017); they are currently under commission to write *HandToMouthToMouthToHand* for the National Theatre's Connections programme. They are the librettist, with Annemarie NíChuirreáin, of Michael Gallen's opera *Elsewheer*, which premiered on the Abbey Stage in 2021, and the sole librettist of *Horse Ape Bird,* an INO and Music Generation co-commission, by David Coonan. They contributed text to THISISPOPBABY's *WAKE*. They were the facilitator of the inaugural WEFT Studio Group, a peer mentorship and support network for Black artists and artists of colour more broadly.

JOHN GUNNING

John is an alumnus of Dublin Youth Theatre and The Lir National Academy of Dramatic Art.

He is a founding member of MALAPROP Theatre. Lighting credits include *Navy Blue* (Oona Doherty) *LOVE+, BlackCatfishMusketeer, JERICHO, Everything Not Saved, Where Sat the Lovers* (MALAPROP)*; Tiny Plays 24/7, Tiny Plays for a Brighter Future* (Fishamble); *Venus in Furs* (Rough Magic SEEDS); *The Roaring Banshees* (Devious Theatre Co.); *We Can't Have Monkeys in the House* (Sad Strippers); *The Three Sisters, Demons* (Lir Academy); *The Egg Is A Lonely Hunter* (Hannah Mamalis). John has toured Ireland and Europe extensively with touring productions. Upcoming work includes lighting design for *MOSH* by Rachel Ní Bhraonáin.

BREFFNI HOLAHAN

Breffni is an actress and theatremaker based in London.

MAEVE O'MAHONY

Maeve is a theatremaker and performer. Stage credits include *The Boy Who Never Was* (Brokentalkers); *An Octoroon* (Abbey Theatre, Irish Times Theatre Awards Best Supporting Actress Nominee);

LOVE+, *Everything Not Saved*, *JERICHO*, *Where Sat the Lovers, Before You Say Anything* (MALAPROP); *White Rabbit Red Rabbit* (Dublin Theatre Festival); *All Honey* (Project Arts Centre); *Outlying Islands, Ethica* (Sugarglass); *Sounds of Wood on Muscle, The Aeneid, Conor: at the end of the Universe* (Collapsing Horse); *Boys & Girls* (59E59, New York); *All Talk* (New Theatre).

Screen credits include the RTÉ Storyland production of *Everything Not Saved*, *Ripper Street* and *Rebecca's Boyfriend*, and narration for the RTÉ series *One Day*. Virtual reality credits include *Intermedial Play* and *Stormy Seas*. She was a participant of the Pan Pan International Mentorship Programme (2019/2020) and holds a BA in Drama & Theatre Studies from Trinity College Dublin.

MOLLY O'CATHAIN

Molly is a set and costume designer based in Dublin, working across theatre, dance, and opera. Molly is a co-founder of MALAPROP Theatre and the designer for their works to date including *Where Sat the Lovers, Before You Say Anything, Everything Not Saved, JERICHO, BlackCatfishMusketeer* and *LOVE+*.

Previous set and costume design credits include *Constellations* (Gate Theatre, Dublin); *Bajazet* for Irish National Opera/ Royal Opera House (nominated for Oliver Award for Best Opera Production); *The Wrens* (Dan Colley); *Haunted* (THISISPOPBABY); *The Playboy of the Western World* (Dublin Theatre Festival/The Gaiety Theatre/The Lyric Belfast); *It Was Easy (in the end)* (The Abbey Theatre/THEATREclub); *Minseach* for Sibeal Davitt Dance, *Ask Too Much of Me* (National Youth Theatre), *La Liberazione di Ruggiero* (Royal Irish Academy of Music); *Serious Money* and *The Ash Fire* (The Lir); *Mr Burns* (Rough Magic).

Costume design credits include *An Octoroon* (Abbey Theatre); *To The Lighthouse* (Co-design, The Everyman/Hatch Productions); *Shit* (THISISPOPBABY); *Recovery* (One Two, One Two). Set design credits include *If These Wigs Could Talk* (THISISPOPBABY); *Absent The Wrong* (The Peacock Theatre) and *Love Songs* by Company Philip Connaghton.

CARLA ROGERS

Carla Rogers is a creative producer and arts marketer with a passion
for supporting artists and teams to make playful, challenging and
thoughtful work, Carla is a founding member of, and producer for,
MALAPROP Theatre. Carla has worked with THISISPOPBABY
since 2017, and has been their lead producer since 2021. She has
worked independently with artists such as Outlandish Theatre,
Sibéal Davitt, Veronica Dyas, and on such festivals as Where We
Live, Live Collision and THE THEATRE MACHINE TURNS
YOU ON Vol. 5.

Select producing credits include *WAKE*, *Party Scene* and tours of
Mark O'Halloran's *Conversations After Sex* (THISISPOPBABY);
Minseach (Sibéal Davitt); *1,000 Miniature Meadows* (Dublin
Fringe Festival 2020); *Not A Funny Word* (tour 2018); *BODIES* film
(Outlandish Theatre/Dublin Film Festival 2022).

Carla has a BA in Modern Irish and Film Studies, and an MA in
Cultural Policy and Arts Management. She is a member of the
steering committee for the National Campaign for the Arts, Ireland.

www.nickhernbooks.co.uk

facebook.com/nickhernbooks

twitter.com/nickhernbooks